The Magic of M

The Magic of Mentoring offers an introduction to the theory and practice of successful mentoring together with a unique focus on how mentors can reflect on the skills they bring to the role, and those they still need to develop. Through the use of scenarios, reflections and stories, the reader is encouraged to apply the content to a real context, demonstrating the importance of reflection for both parties and the benefits derived from this, especially those related to understanding ourselves and others.

Written by Carol Thompson, who has worked with a range of trainee teachers and mentors, this book draws from the author's own experience to explore the importance of self-development, and the ways in which this can be enhanced through practice. Reviewing key themes in relation to mentoring, including models and current practice, it considers the creation of a nurturing environment through effective communication as well as acknowledging the need to generate the right challenge for mentees. All aspects of mentoring are outlined, emphasising how personal development can improve the experience of your mentees, build your own confidence, enhance your transferable skills, and advance your own professional practice and relationships. Engaging activities are provided for mentors to undertake to support their own professional development.

The Magic of Mentoring is an ideal guide for all those studying coaching or mentoring on a formal programme or for anyone who mentors others in formal or informal settings. The structure of 15 concise chapters lends itself to referencing back and targeted reading for specific guidance.

Carol Thompson is a Senior Lecturer in Teacher Education and Mentoring. Carol has had a range of teaching and management roles within the further education sector and for the past 10 years has been training teachers and mentors within the department of Teacher Education at the University of Bedfordshire. In addition she is an active researcher and a Fellow of the Further Education Trust for Leadership.

The Magic of Mentoring

Developing Others and Yourself

Carol Thompson

Routledge
Taylor & Francis Group

LONDON AND NEW YORK

First edition published 2019
by Routledge
2 Park Square, Milton Park, Abingdon, Oxon, OX14 4RN

and by Routledge
52 Vanderbilt Avenue, New York, NY 10017

Routledge is an imprint of the Taylor & Francis Group, an informa business

© 2019 Carol Thompson

British Library Cataloguing-in-Publication Data
A catalogue record for this book is available from the British Library

Library of Congress Cataloging-in-Publication Data
A catalog record has been requested for this book

ISBN: 978-1-138-30965-4 (hbk)
ISBN: 978-1-138-30966-1 (pbk)
ISBN: 978-1-315-14347-7 (ebk)

Typeset in Galliard
by Swales & Willis Ltd

MIX
Paper from
responsible sources
FSC FSC® C013056
www.fsc.org

Printed and bound in Great Britain by
TJ International Ltd, Padstow, Cornwall

Contents

Contents

Acknowledgements

To the teachers and mentors who provided opportunities for me to connect somewhat random ideas and to my students who taught me most of what I know – thank you. To those patient, special people who listened to my ramblings, kept back-up copies of my work and had continued faith in my ability to complete this book, it probably wouldn't have happened without you. Finally, to Professor Janice Wearmouth who introduced me to my publishers and to Routledge for taking a leap of faith in me.

The magic of mentoring

Introduction

Historically, being allocated the role of apprentice to a magician or master craftsman was a way to develop skills that would result in the ability to earn a living. In many professions this practice is still highly valued, with apprentices learning from, and being guided by, experienced 'elders'. Within fiction, these relationships also thrive and provide an opportunity to move a plot from one scene to the next. This often happens when the mentor says or does something that inspires change, or through some action teaches an important lesson. Books such as the *Harry Potter* series and *The Lord of the Rings*' trilogy provide strong examples of this and feature charismatic mentors in the form of Dumbledore and Gandalf. Gandalf, acknowledged as the wisest of the Istari, is also known for his ability to ask insightful questions and in the *Harry Potter* stories, Albus Dumbledore can cast spells that outwit opponents and can defeat dark wizards in duels. But perhaps his most important skill is his ability to drop pearls of wisdom that in themselves are *magic*. As Dumbledore suggests 'Words are, in my not-so-humble opinion, our most inexhaustible source of magic. Capable of both inflicting injury, and remedying it.'[1]

Throughout the *Harry Potter* series, Dumbledore imparts his wisdom through both words and actions; he is at all times the master who openly shares his skills; subsequently, his apprentice observes, imitates and develops his competencies until he too is proficient in the art of magic.

A seemingly less dramatic but not dissimilar example is the way in which mentors and mentees work together. The mentoring process is evident within a range of occupational settings such as education, medicine and business; in some cases it is a structured and formal role, whereas in others it is simply the result of serendipity. Either way, the process can be at the root of significant change for mentees, something that could be described as *magical* and not unlike the relationship between the magician and the apprentice.

The process of mentoring is usually viewed as something that encourages developmental change for mentees; what is less obvious is the changes that often take place for the mentors involved in these relationships. Through exploring the role and reflecting on their own practice in order to support their mentees, mentors are also involved in their own transformation. Becoming a mentor is a process in which you have the opportunity to explore your ontology and, according to Owen, develop a greater awareness that: 'change is always possible, that there is always more than one perspective, and that the essence of useful change lies in having both creativity and access to a greater number of choices' (Owen 2001:xi).

In this book, a democratic model of mentoring is explored, within which positive change for both mentors and mentees is acknowledged and actively encouraged. It is based on experiences of training mentors and includes the information you would expect to find in any educational programme that has a focus on coaching or mentoring. However, experience has taught me that the best mentor development does not restrict itself to conveying information about theoretical models or providing templates for practice. Instead it includes deep self-reflection about current beliefs, values and practice. For this reason I have included some stories, activities or reflection points in each of the chapters. In doing so, there is an awareness that such activities are not always viewed with enthusiasm – after all, you probably bought a book because you wanted to be told how to *do* mentoring, and of course there will be content that meets that need. In support of this approach I draw on the work of Alfred Korzybski (1933) and the well-known phrase 'The map is not the territory'. This was originally used to describe the relationship between an object and a representation of that object and, in common usage, it illustrates the concept that the way we see the world isn't necessarily *reality*.

The route to becoming a mentor is quite unique and, as such, there is no single path or direct map to follow. Perhaps the most important thing is that the process will involve being open to new experiences and able to reflect honestly on your own skills and abilities. This book, and the activities within it, should help you to do that because it will be completely personal to you. A basic map of mentoring can be provided but the intention here is to produce something that I hope will be a more of a guide for the unique journey you will follow in your own mentoring practice.

The book is structured in such a way that you can use it as a step-by-step approach to developing your knowledge and skills, or a tool that you can 'dip into' when you want to explore a specific aspect of mentoring. We start by considering the basics such as models of mentoring and ways of creating a suitable environment, including appropriate boundaries. This is followed by closer examination of things that may impact on mentoring practice such as emotional intelligence and the importance of behavioural flexibility. The mentor's role as something of a 'conduit' for change is recognised throughout the book and we explore the importance of modelling excellence and challenging mentees by providing the constructive feedback that will inform the development of suitably challenging goals. Finally, we will consider typical dilemmas faced by mentors and how you might use the strategies outlined in the book to help you overcome these.

In every chapter there are skills you can adopt to improve your mentoring practice but all of this is offered in the knowledge that *you* are the person most informed about your context and as such will have all the resources you need to select which approaches will be of benefit to you. Extending your knowledge and skill range simply increases your choices and allows you greater flexibility to take more creative approaches. I hope that this book provides a useful and interesting guide, perhaps even a vague map – but something that most certainly allows you to discover your own territory.

Note

1 *Harry Potter and the Deathly Hallows*, directed by Yates (2011; Burbank, CA: Warner Home Video, 2011), DVD.

References

Korzybski, A. (1933) *Science and Sanity, An Introduction to Non-Aristotelian Systems and General Semantics.* : The International Non-Aristotelian Library Pub. Co., pp. 747–761.

Owen, N. (2001) *The Magic of Metaphor, 77 Stories for Teachers, Trainers & Thinkers.* Carmarthen: Crown House Publishing.

The roots of mentoring

What is the first thing that comes to mind when you think about a tree? Do you consider how green the leaves are, or how many branches it has? Or perhaps look at the trunk and imagine how long it has been in position and all the things it must have witnessed in that time? For most of us observation will focus on the things above the surface of the ground; we may be struck by the tree's beauty or marvel at how proud and tall it stands, but very rarely do we consider what is keeping it in place – trees must develop deep roots in order to grow and flourish.

At its best, the impact of mentoring can be life-changing. It can represent a relationship that inspires mutual learning and growth and has the capacity to transform individuals and organisations. At its worst it is a relationship that pays 'lip-service' to a process, or something that 'looks good on paper', potentially with both parties being coerced into participating. In a culture of high accountability, providing evidence that we support colleagues, students and community members through a mentoring programme is an attractive prospect, which may result in the development of mentoring approaches that focus on the superficial but do not have strong roots or the capacity to bloom and grow. In this chapter we explore the roots of mentoring, by which I mean the fundamental principles underpinning any model of mentoring, the core values assumed by mentors, and the ways in which mentoring can become a democratic process and create a culture where both mentors and mentees will thrive.

What is a mentor?

There are many definitions of mentoring which in turn inform our vision of what a mentor should 'look' like. A brief scan of history outlines some influential mentor–mentee relationships, including musicians, business-men and political figures; for example, Ray Charles was mentored by music industry legend Quincy Jones, Bill Gates by American business magnate Warren Buffet and Carl Jung by Sigmund Freud.

Within all of these examples the role of mentoring is depicted as a relationship wherein the development of the mentee is the key focus and the mentors are the altruistic providers of expert guidance and support who freely give their time and share their knowledge. Indeed the name 'mentor' derives from one of the characters in Homer's *Odyssey* – 'Mentor' – who, when the King of Ithaca (Odysseus) went off to war, was entrusted with the care of his son Telemachus. The very nature of this relationship suggests that the trusted must at all times be responsive to the needs of the trustee in much the same way as within a parent and child relationship. Such portrayals of mentor–mentee rela-tionships depict the mentor as an older, more experienced advisor or a more knowledgeable, and perhaps higher status, role model guiding a protégé, a description that is similar to Erikson's theory of generativity whereby an older person chooses to nurture the things that will outlast them, and in doing so encourages a continuation of something that has begun but cannot be finished within a single lifetime (Erikson 1959). However, there is a key difference in the motivation associated with these descriptions; in the first example there is no reference to what a mentor might get out of the relationship, whereas the latter clearly recognises the self-interest apparent in a sense of 'self-reproduction', as Freud (n.d.) acknowledged when referring to Jung as his 'heir' or 'successor': 'If I am Moses, then you are Joshua and will take possession of the promised land of psychiatry, which I shall only be able to glimpse from afar' (Letter to Carl Jung, January 17, 1909).

Alternative definitions of mentoring refer to a development activity within organisations or someone who helps an individual to achieve career aims. The title is used in a number of ways and it seems that, to arrive at a useful definition, we must also have an understanding of context. The role of the mentor differs according to why and where it evolved and ways of being a mentor seem to vary according to individual interpretation – perhaps that is how it should be. One definition that seems to fit most mentoring roles is this: 'A mentor is a person who helps another to think things through' (Pask 2004, cited in Pask and Joy 2007:8). In this definition the mentor does not assume superior knowledge or status but acts more as a channel through which the mentee can develop their own approaches. It is also possible that the process of helping another to think things through, perhaps by questioning accepted wisdom, assists the mentor in developing their own thinking and as such it becomes a symbiotic relationship.

Mentoring versus coaching

A further confusion in defining the mentoring role occurs when we make reference to coaching and mentoring. These are words that are often used together, sometimes interchangeably and, as stated by Lancer et al., there is confusion over definitions 'What one group describes as coaching, another would perceive as mentoring. This arises due to the complexity of coaching and mentoring and the plethora of different approaches' (Lancer et al. 2016:5).

The Chartered Institute of Personnel and Development (CIPD) describes coaching as 'Developing a person's skills and knowledge so that their job performance improves' (CIPD 2004:online). This appears to indicate a form of specific training and would certainly be in keeping with the sort of coaching we might associate with sports training, its focus being to improve performance or to reach specific goals. Although not my working definition, the term 'mentor' is also used in some contexts to describe the role of someone whose job it is to ensure that the performance of others is up to the organisation's required standard in a given skill, and thereby describes a role that we can presume involves the utilisation of a number of coaching skills.

The purpose of mentoring has been described as a relationship: 'To support and encourage people to manage their own learning in order that they may maximise their potential, develop their skills, improve their performance and become the person they want to be' (Parsloe 2008:online). This description illustrates a process that develops capability in a general sense, rather than having a focus on the acquisition of specific skills and one that is driven by the mentee rather than the mentor.

Traditionally, mentoring is seen as a more long-term relationship based on trust and authenticity, in which knowledge is openly shared. Within this framework, and through their prior experience, mentors are able to make the hazy clear and the impossible possible and, according to Jung, the mentor symbolises knowledge, reflection, insight, wisdom, cleverness and intuition (Jung 1958).

When is a coach a mentor?

Consider the list in Table 1.1 and think about whether you would believe the statements relate to the role of a coach or of a mentor. The columns are mixed up, so the easiest way to work through this is to add 'C' or 'M' next to each statement to indicate your choice.

Table 1.1 Statements relating to the role of coach and mentor

Ongoing relationship that can last for a long time	Relationship generally has a short duration
Generally more structured in nature and meetings scheduled on a regular basis	Can be more informal and meetings can take place as and when the mentored individual needs some guidance and or support
Short term (sometimes time bounded) and focused on specific development areas/issues	More long term and takes a broader view of the person
Role holder usually passes on experience and is normally more senior in the organisation	Not generally performed on the basis that role holder needs direct experience of client's formal occupational role

(continued)

Table 1.1 (*continued*)

The focus is on career and personal development	Focus generally on development/issues at work
Agenda is set by the 'protégé', with the role holder providing support and guidance to prepare them for future roles	Agenda focused on achieving specific, immediate goals
Revolves more around developing the protégé professionally	Revolves more around specific development areas/issues

You can find the answers to this activity at the end of the chapter, but it is worth remembering that this is only a viewpoint on the differences between the two roles. Within your own context and mentoring relationship, it is very likely that aspects of both definitions apply. A mentor may well be defined as someone who helps another person's thinking but in most scenarios they are also part of the process of helping the other to achieve their aims and in this sense take on aspects of both roles.

Models of mentoring

As with most models it is useful to employ your own judgement, using your knowledge and experience of the context in which your mentoring will take place. Many people will view models of mentoring with a certain amount of cynicism because it is difficult to take a 'one-size-fits-all' approach in any single relationship. However, reviewing the ideas of others is in itself a useful activity and will allow you to start to develop your own views on what the mentoring role should involve.

One model that acknowledges the blurring of boundaries between mentoring and coaching activities is that presented by Pask and Joy (2007) (Figure 1.1). In this model colour coding is used to acknowledge the relevance of each part of the process, for example, the contracting and evidence phases are shown as neutral because these can apply to all stages.

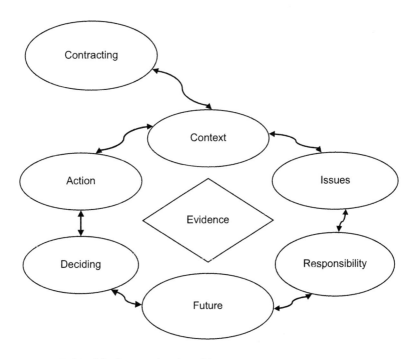

Figure 1.1 Model of mentoring/coaching

The other steps follow an enhanced traffic light system, so stage 1 is 'green for go', stage 2 amber/yellow, to indicate the need for caution, and stage 3 is red to indicate a 'stop' until there is evidence to show that the mentee wants to make changes. Stages 4 and 5 are shown as blue, to indicate 'blue skies thinking' which is considered important in the ideas stage and the final stage is shown in purple, to represent the 'purple patch' normally associated with notable success (Pask and Joy 2007:13). Significance is also given to the name of the model which uses a long dash to connect the words mentoring and coaching.

An alternative model is provided by Clutterbuck (2004), in which different dimensions of the mentoring relationship are acknowledged. These include the directive and non-directive nature of the mentor's role and raise questions about who should guide the path of the relationship. Clutterbuck suggests that, when the outcomes are related to personal development, the most effective relationships are when the mentee takes control, but acknowledges that the opposite may be true when the relationship has a focus on sponsorship, whereby a sponsor (usually someone senior in the organisation) actively promotes a protégé in order to help advance their career. In doing so, the sponsor is able to benefit from the protégé's efforts as well as be seen as a leader who can spot potential. The model also acknowledges that the mentor's role includes both nurturing and stretching, requiring a range of skills to enable the most appropriate intervention at relevant points in the relationship. Added to these dimensions are the 'four basic styles of helping' which outline the behaviours recognised in 'helping to learn'. A simple depiction of a model including the dimensions and four basic styles of helping is shown in Figure 1.2.

A popular model within business and the education sector is the GROW model (Whitmore 2009) which is a simple framework for structuring the mentoring relationship. The acronym stands for:

(G)oals (R)eality (O)ptions (W)ill

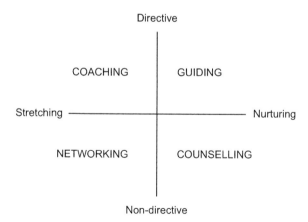

Figure 1.2 Four basic styles of helping (including dimensions of learning)

The aim is to provide a four-stage model that raises awareness of aspirations, possibilities and potential actions to achieve specific goals, and encourages focus on how much a particular outcome is desired by considering the 'Will' element of the model. The basis of this model is grounded in coaching philosophy because it has a strong focus on achieving specific outcomes, which may explain its popularity in commercial settings. The simplicity of the model is also appealing for those working in situations in which their role involves supporting several individuals, for example in an educational setting.

One concern with such a focus on specificity is the possibility that it may also lead to a limitation of the mentee's potential because setting specific goals through the use of any model limits their scope by default. For example, if we were to use the GROW approach, we immediately start with the Goal set in the context of our current Reality; then we would consider the options to create a way forward. In itself this may be a useful process, but it is also worth considering what experiences have led to the formulation of a specific goal. Has this decision been based on what we want to achieve or is it based on what others, for example managers, colleagues or partners, want from us? This of course does not reject the value of setting goals and targets; in fact research would suggest that there is indeed a benefit to this process (Latham and Locke 2007).

A simple model of mentoring based on three stages is outlined by Alred et al. (1998) This model emphasises the importance of the 'helping' aspect of the mentor's role and considers:

- Exploration
- New understanding
- Action planning (Alred et al. 1998).

This approach aims to put the mentee in the 'driving seat' by using a series of questions to elicit information, reframe understanding and generate action planning in an attempt to solve whatever concerns the mentee brings to the meeting. The process is based on Egan's Skilled Helper Model which is explored further in Chapter 8. This was developed to help people solve problems as well as create opportunities for action, and is succinctly defined as 'a way of helping people become better at helping themselves in their everyday lives' (Egan 1998:7).

Key principles of mentoring

Mentoring has been described as: 'a supportive relationship; a helping process; a teaching–learning process; a reflective process; a career development process; a formalised process and a role constructed by or for a mentor' Roberts (2000:145). The role serves a number of purposes from the pragmatic to the more idealistic. Mentors are proactive in supporting others towards achieving their goals; they also act as role models and in a work context may have a significant influence in helping to form a mentee's professional identity. Mentoring creates a relationship in which experimentation leads to learning through analysis, reflection on situations, practice, successes and mistakes. The relationship involves a real connection in which openness and honesty create a strong bond and an environment in which both parties can be themselves. This provides a safe space for the mentee to learn and grow, alongside an opportunity for the mentor to nurture that growth while developing further understanding of their own strengths and gaps in learning.

Although we may each adopt a different model to inform our mentoring practice, there are some key aspects to mentoring that should be considered. These become apparent when we remind ourselves that mentoring is a relationship and as such requires a connection between the mentor and mentee. As suggested by Klasen and Clutterbuck (2002), trust is an important component of this because it provides an opportunity for open and honest communication between both parties. In addition to this we might also include confidentiality, mutual respect and sensitivity to others' feelings.

Within formal settings, such as education and the workplace, mentoring tends to be viewed as a structured process in which the focus of dialogue is to encourage reflection in the mentee. In this context a key principle of the mentoring relationship would also be based on agreed boundaries that acknowledge each person's role within it. The principles of mentoring may be informed by a number of things, which are adapted according to the context but could include:

- The development of a relationship based on trust and mutual respect
- A focus on learning that leads to change
- An agenda set by the mentee rather than the mentor
- A commitment to supporting the development of individual goals before organisational goals
- The ability to encourage learning and change through the empowerment of the mentee
- A foundation of ethical practice that safeguards all parties.

It could be said that a mentor's overall role is to nurture the mentee in a way that supports them to become whatever they aspire to be. If this is to be a truly developmental process then the relationship must allow space for reflection and analysis which provides the opportunity to de-construct experiences honestly, potentially 'developing an awareness of new information and creating dissonance with the current position' Timberley et al. (2007: xv). This suggests the need for open and critical dialogue within a relationship of trust and the provision of a 'critical space' in which mentors and mentees can develop reflective thinking (Cherian 2007). In this sense, effective mentoring could be described as a 'duet' in which both mentor and mentee discuss each other's success and issues in order to formulate appropriate approaches to whatever challenges are presented.

A first step in creating this type of collegiate culture is to establish our own values in relation to the purpose and practice of mentoring. Values could be described as guidelines for how we choose to conduct our lives, and for some they are based on ingrained beliefs about how life *should* be. Our core values are the principles that shape our behaviour and our thoughts, and as a result have a very strong influence on our attitudes and beliefs. Think about the following situations:

1) Sally is a teacher working with adult learners. She is very dedicated to her job and takes a genuine personal pride in her role and in the way she supports her students to achieve their academic goals. Sally has many years' experience and is very confident that her 'no nonsense' philosophy about teaching and learning is at the root of her success. You have been working with one of Sally's groups who have complained that they find her rather intimidating, so much so that they are afraid to ask questions in class and feel they are being swept along with the lessons without really learning anything. You know that Sally will be very upset to hear this news but you are concerned about what the students have told you. What do you do?

2) You have just started a new job in a small family business. When looking at the weekly accounts you notice that the petty cash tin seems to be down by £100. You then find out that one of your colleagues has been borrowing money from the petty cash in order to buy food for his family. He tells you that his wife has lost her job and they are really struggling week by week and that he puts the money back as soon as he is paid. You believe that he does return the money. What do you do?

In both these situations it is likely that the decision you arrive at will be informed by your own values and these in turn will guide your actions.

Consider the A–Z of values and highlight any that are important to you (Table 1.2). When you have done that, try to select three as your core values.

Table 1.2 Common values in mentoring: the A–Z

A	B	C
Accuracy	Boldness	Challenge
Acknowledgement	Beingness	Compassion
Authenticity	Benevolence	Creativity

(continued)

Table 1.2 (*continued*)

D	E	F
Diligence	Empathy	Freedom
Diversity	Empowerment	Fairness
Discovery	Enthusiasm	Flexibility
G	H	I
Generosity	Honesty	Independence
Geniality	Humour	Integrity
Goodwill	Happiness	Idealism
J	K	L
Joy	Kindness	Leadership
Justice	Knowledge	Learning
Jubilance	Keenness	Love
M	N	O
Merit	Nurturing	Optimism
Mindfulness	Naturalness	Openness
Motivation		Originality
P	Q	R
Patience	Quietness	Reliability
Productivity	Quiescence	Respect
Professionalism	Quality	Risk taking
S	T	U
Self-confidence	Trust	Understanding
Spirituality	Truth	Unconditional positive regard
Success	Transformation	Unification
V	W	X
Vitality	Wit	Xenophilia[a]
Versatility	Willingness	Xenodochial[b]
Virtue	Wisdom	
Y	Z	
(Being) Young at heart	Zealousness	
Yes-ability		

a A xenophile is somebody who likes the people, customs and culture of other countries and could be considered to be open to and appreciative of diversity.
b Xenodochial is an adjective describing something such as a person or place that is friendly to strangers.

A democratic approach

A key challenge for mentors is the promotion of a democratic approach as opposed to a hierarchical one. By representing the mentoring relationship as a shared experience between professionals, rather than the more traditional master and apprentice model, the focus shifts from an unequal to a more balanced relationship and moves towards an emphasis on creating the right environment for change as opposed to instruction on what or how to change. In some ways this is similar to Roger's person-centred approach to counselling whereby the attention is focussed not on 'treating' or 'changing' another but on providing the right environment for growth (Rogers 1961).

Applying this notion to mentoring would advocate a model in which mentors and mentees work together to facilitate change, thereby removing mentors from the pedestal that labels them as 'expert' and creating a relationship based on mutual respect and trust. In this way mentors can open up their own practice to scrutiny and recognise that they too have much to learn, thereby facilitating a situation in which the mentor's personal development is also enhanced.

The creation of a democratic framework in mentoring is a way of acknowledging that all parties within a relationship bring something to it and recognises the benefits of collaboration within a community of professionals. It represents a form of collaborative, rather than master–servant, apprenticeship, which supports learning through reciprocal interactions by placing equal value on both the mentor's and the mentee's participation.

It is suggested that the role of the mentor is a complex balance of inspiring, challenging, supporting and counselling. At the heart of a democratic approach is the core belief that this is a relationship from which both parties can benefit. Being involved in mentoring is a way in which we can share our expertise but if the process ends there then we are in danger of stagnating any future development. As suggested by Stephen Spielberg (see www.brainyquote.com/quotes/quotes/s/stevenspie584069.html): 'The delicate balance of mentoring someone is not creating them in your own image but giving them the opportunity to create themselves.'

The metaphor of a tree can be used to describe a democratic model of mentoring. The roots are grounded within a sound theoretical base that reflects the mentor's knowledge and experience. At its core are the key values that form the framework of a mentor–mentee relationship; these include nurturing an open and honest communication style built on trust between both parties. It also acknowledges the emotional and social support required to sustain mentees along the journey from novice to expert. Although it is recognised that mentors act as role models for their mentees and, as such, the expectation is that they display techniques and behaviours that represent good practice, it is also suggested that the role of *expert* is removed in order to avoid the danger of replicating another's approach unquestioningly. From these strong roots, firm branches of practice can develop and lead to the blossoming of learning through reciprocal interaction.

A sprinkling of magic

In a way, the practice of mentoring is a form of magic. It helps to transform the mentee from novice to expert, but, unlike the magician who waves a wand or casts a spell, the mentor has more in common with the alchemist. A mentor creates the conditions in which a mentee can thrive. Alongside this the mentor provides guidance that enhances technical skill and the ability to reflect on and refine professional practice. All of this helps mentors and mentees to become part of a structure that supports, inspires – and transforms.

The application of a democratic approach to mentoring ensures that it becomes a two-way process, with the mentor having as much to gain as the mentee. A key to this is a foundation on which both partners are seen as equals despite differences in age or experience. Initially the mentor may be the one to take the initiative to get things going but the process should also involve a gradual 'letting go' of power, so that both mentor and mentee develop autonomously.

Adopting a model to inform your mentoring practice provides a framework to structure the relationship but does not offer the roots from which mentoring will develop. It could be considered more akin to a rabbit guard (Figure 1.3), in that it offers an initial defence to protect what is new and delicate, and stops indecision nibbling away at thoughts about how to conduct the relationship. At the same time, it provides a supporting framework which allows strong roots to grow.

Figure 1.3 A sprinkling of magic: rabbit guard

Table 1.3 Answers to activities: coach or mentor?

Mentor	Coach
Ongoing relationship that can last for a long time	Relationship generally has a short duration
Can be more informal and meetings can take place as and when the mentored individual needs some guidance and or support	Generally more structured in nature and meetings scheduled on a regular basis
More long term and takes a broader view of the person	Short term (sometimes time bounded) and focused on specific development areas/issues
Role holder usually passes on experience and is normally more senior in the organisation	Not generally performed on the basis that role holder needs direct experience of client's formal occupational role
The focus is on career and personal development	Focus generally on development/issues at work
Agenda is set by the protégé, with the role holder providing support and guidance to prepare them for future roles	Agenda focused on achieving specific, immediate goals
Revolves more around developing the protégé professionally	Revolves more around specific development areas/issues

There is no magical formula to ensure the success of mentoring, but giving thought to our approach, values, attitudes and beliefs allows us to undertake the role with confidence and congruence. This chapter has outlined definitions and principles of mentoring and explored some popular models that can inform your practice. By applying this information mindfully it is possible to discover the magic, whatever that might be in your specific context.

Suggested further reading

Clutterbuck, D. (2004) *Everyone Needs a Mentor: Fostering Talent in Your Organisation* (4th edn.) London: Chartered Institute of Personnel and Development.

References

Alred, G., Garvey, B. and Smith, R. (1998) *Mentoring Pocketbook*. Alresford: Management Pocketbooks.

Chartered Institute of Personnel and Development. (2004) *Coaching and Buying Coaching Services. Guide*. London: CIPD. Available at: www.cipd.co.uk/guides [date accessed 15 November 2017].

Cherian, F. (2007) Learning to Teach: Teacher Candidates Reflect on the Relational, Conceptual and Contextual Influences of Responsive Mentorship. *Canadian Journal of Education*, 30: 25–46.

Clutterbuck, D. (2004) *Everyone Needs a Mentor: Fostering Talent in Your Organisation* (4th edn.) London: Chartered Institute of Personnel and Development.

Egan, G. (1998) *The Skilled Helper: A Problem Management Approach to Helping*. Boston, MA: Brooks-Cole.

Erikson, E. H. (1959) *Identity and the Life Cycle*. New York: International Universities Press.

Freud, S. (n.d.) Sigmund Freud Quotes. Quotes.net. Available at: https://quotes.net/quote6397.

Jung, C. J. (1958) *Psyche and Symbol*. New York: Doubleday.

Klasen, K. and Clutterbuck, D. (2002) *Implementing Mentoring Schemes; A Practical Guide to Successful Programmes*. London: Butterworth-Heinemann.

Lancer, N., Clutterbuck, D. and Megginson, D. (2016) *Techniques for Coaching and Mentoring* (2nd edn.) Oxon: Routledge.

Latham, G. P. and Locke, E. A. (2007) New Developments in and Directions for Goalsetting Research. *European Psychologist*, 12(4): 29–300.

Parsloe, E. (2008). MentorSET. Available at: www.mentorset.org.uk/pages/mentoring.htm [date accessed 14 November 2017].

Pask, R. and Joy, B. (2007) *Mentoring–Coaching a Guide for Education Professionals*. London: Open University Press.

Roberts, A. (2000) Mentoring Revisited: A Phenomenological Reading of the Literature. *Mentoring Tutoring*, 8: 145–170.

Rogers, C. (1961) *On Becoming a Person: A Therapist's View of Psychotherapy*. New York: Houghton Mifflin.

Timberley, H., Wilson, A., Barrar, H. and Fung, I. (2007) *Teacher Professional Learning and Development, Best Evidence Synthesis Iteration (BES)*. Wellington, New Zealand: Ministry of Education.

Whitmore, J. (2009) *Coaching for Performance, GROWing Human Potential and Purpose, The Principles and Practice of Coaching and Leadership* (4th edn.) London: Nicholas Brealey Publishing.

Creating the right environment

How do you encourage a tree to grow strong and bloom? Do you focus on providing adequate nourishment or try to control the micro-climate it inhabits? Is it best to provide the support of a stake, or to allow the tree to develop its own knots and twists? Trees need sustenance to grow but we don't buy them food, instead they make their own through water, sunlight and nutrients in the soil. Usually trees do not grow beyond their ability to support themselves; given the right conditions they are strong and independent and live in harmony with their environment.

In this chapter, we explore the environment of mentoring, the factors that have an impact on the effectiveness of a mentoring relationship, including the 'situatedness' of mentor and mentee learning, the past experiences that have an influence on current practice, and the ways in which rapport and acceptance can be used to generate a positive climate for change.

Situated learning

Within our culture, it is easy to assume that learning takes place within formalised structures. We learn at school, college and university. Learning has a clear beginning and end, and usually a recognisable outcome which is often dependent on teaching and testing. Most curricula and classrooms are designed on the basis of these assumptions and in this way learning becomes something we do separately to other parts of our lives. Unlike traditional, classroom-based learning, situated learning normally occurs within its natural context, for example we learn how to communicate from our families, we learn about a new job from our colleagues, and we absorb cultural learning through interactions that are common within our cultural and social environments. In contrast to classroom-based learning, which is usually out of context and somewhat abstract, situated learning is firmly placed within a given framework, which informs the meaning we assign to it (Lave 1988). In this sense, learning is not seen as an acquisition of knowledge but as the result of participation in social interaction and collaboration, whereby learners become involved in social groups that embody certain behaviours and beliefs.

Communities of practice

A different perspective to traditional learning is offered by Lave and Wenger (1991) who used the term 'community of practice' to describe the ways in which learning takes place through social interaction in communities of common interest and collaboration.

According to Wenger (n.d.) there are three characteristics that are common to communities of practice. These include the *domain*, which refers to an area of common interest, the *community*, which describes the way in which interests are pursued through joint activities, discussion and sharing information, and *practice*, which specifies the area of practice community members are involved in. The choice of words is deliberate because it specifies that community members are practitioners who have a repertoire of resources to bring to the community. This makes the terms particularly applicable to professional groups, for example a community of engineers, nurses or teachers rather than friendship groups or people with a shared interest in a hobby such as a reading group.

Communities of practice might also be described as communities of learning because they provide an opportunity for members to collaborate by sharing knowledge and resources, as well as creating a forum for discussing ideas. As such they can be a unique asset to mentees who may be new to an organisation or professional group. One key consideration is how mentees might be introduced to a particular community, a process that can be supported effectively by a mentor through 'legitimate peripheral participation' (Lave and Wenger 1991). This term describes the ways in which individuals begin to integrate into specific communities, initially by taking tentative steps, perhaps supported by another, until they are able to participate fully and in turn enrich the community by sharing their own knowledge and skills.

One distinct advantage of introducing mentees to communities of practice is the opportunity to expand the professional circle beyond the mentoring connection. Mentors usually operate in a particular context, and the guidance and expertise they offer will most likely relate to that situation. This has the benefit of being able to offer specific, and often tested, direction but, at the same time, the very nature of this form of situated learning also has the potential to constrain development so in a sense mentors are both supported and inhibited by their experience. This is not to say that sharing this experience is not valuable; quite the opposite would be true. It is simply an acknowledgement that both mentors and mentees need to develop greater awareness of themselves and their professional practice if they are to continue to grow in a way that allows independence to develop, alongside a harmonious integration into the community.

Learning in this way means we are continually evolving: we learn through our participation and we enrich the environment by the new perspectives we might bring to it.

Self-awareness

Life scripts

According to the theory of transactional analysis (TA) each of us writes a story of our lives when we are children. This story has a basic plot developed in our infant years and is embellished later in childhood and adolescence. As adults, we are probably not consciously aware of the story but we live it out faithfully nevertheless! In TA theory, this is known as our life script (Stewart and Joines 2003). A life script provides a blueprint for our life, mapping out expectations and encouraging behaviours that lead us towards getting what we expect.

Meisha's story

Meisha struggled to maintain long-term relationships. She didn't understand why but for some reason, whenever she got close to someone, they pulled away from her. Meisha knew that there must be something about her that put others off but couldn't pinpoint it; she felt she was attractive and fun to be around and she cared about the people she was close too – if they stayed around long enough for her to care.

It seemed to Meisha that she was doomed to fail in romance. To Meisha this also seemed to reflect other aspects of her life where she didn't feel she was a successful as she should be. She was beginning to wonder if she should take the same approach to her relationships as she did with the other things she wasn't good at – stop trying.

What Meisha was less aware of was her tendency to sabotage her interactions with others because she was anticipating failure. She was very good at taking comments as criticism and picking fights in order to test loved ones. After all, they were going to leave her anyway so why not pre-empt the inevitable?

This example outlines a life script based on Meisha's belief that she is not good enough. This particular story may have developed out of one or more events, but at some point in Meisha's life a decision was made that she was somehow inferior or flawed and, as a result, other people would not want to be around her. Over the years Meisha had learnt a number of behaviours that served as a form of protection, such as not doing things she expected to fail at or giving people reasons to question their relationship with her. Without being fully aware of it, Meisha was playing out the story she had composed about her life.

Narrative identity

The theory of narrative identity also refers to the way in which we internalise our 'stories' in creating a sense of self. Such stories are based on an integration of a reconstructed past, perceived present and predicted future in a way that provides us with a unified narrative. This develops through our experiences and interactions with caregivers and the process involved in the construction of our autobiographical memories. Researchers have linked this to conversations between parents and young children and the sophisticated meaning-making process we use to make sense of certain periods of our lives, therefore: 'Through narrative identity, people convey to themselves and to others who they are now, how they came to be, and where they think their lives may be going in the future' (McAdams and McClean 2013:233).

In this way, our stories become the foundation of our personalities and influence the way we work, think about ourselves and interact with others. For these reasons our stories are important in helping us to become more self-aware, which in turn may increase our ability to adapt to a range of situations; as Socrates decreed 'Know thyself'. According to researchers, narrative identity formulates in late adolescence/early adulthood as thinking matures and individuals are able to provide answers to key life questions such as 'Who am I?', 'How did my life come to be?' and 'Where am I going?' (Erikson 1994; McAdams 1985).

Given the ways in which life stories evolve and narrative identities emerge, it would be foolish to assume that change is something that would be effected easily, or indeed that significant change was necessarily a requirement of the mentoring role. The ability to implement changes will vary on an individual basis but, for any change to take place, it is important for both mentors and mentees to generate a greater sense of awareness of their own stories in order to work more effectively with each other and in the wider community.

> Think about your early life story – what people, events and experiences have had the greatest influence on you?

> How do these people, events and experience influence the way you think about life, work and yourself?

Becoming self-aware isn't something we can simply switch on and it won't happen immediately. However, developing the practice of reflection, introspection and openness will increase your ability to be self-aware and make conscious decisions about your actions and interactions.

The importance of rapport

What is rapport?

The success of any interaction with another person will be largely determined by the amount of rapport generated. This does not mean that you have to be 'best friends' with everyone who crosses your path, but it does mean giving some thought to factors that will help or inhibit communication.

Rapport describes a harmonious liaison between people who feel they have a sense of connection, so its basis is founded on mutual attentiveness, positivity, and the generation of the feeling that the conversation and participants are 'in sync'. According to Lancer et al. (2016) there are five components to good rapport:

1. Trust
2. Focus
3. Empathy
4. Congruence
5. Empowerment.

We generally feel we have rapport with those people we like and trust, something that is more easily built when behaviour is congruent with our expectations of the situation and the relationship. If someone shows empathy this enables us to feel heard, and having a focus ensures that there is mutual attentiveness within a conversation, but how do we generate rapport with people we don't know particularly well? And how much rapport should we have?

Creating rapport

There is no foolproof way of creating rapport with another person and generating a set of guidelines may suggest that there is a 'one-size-fits-all' approach, something that by its very nature reduces human communication to a mechanistic, rather than a relational, process. However, it is possible to draw some generalisations from behaviours which usually help to generate a sense of being in tune with another. The following outlines some of these behaviours, alongside some additional considerations:

- Leaning towards and making eye contact with the other person to show that you are focused on what they have to say. Remember that personal boundaries vary between individuals and too much eye contact can be intimidating. It is also important to be aware of cultural differences and what may or may not be considered appropriate.

- Smiling and using 'reinforcers' such as nodding and gestures to provide positive feedback when the other person is talking. This should be genuine, so avoid providing positive feedback if it is something you don't agree with – it is also important to generate trust by knowing and being true to your own views.

- Building on the other person's ideas to show that you are listening to them. This can be done by paraphrasing, reflecting back, and adding questions or ideas. Remember to build on ideas, not bulldoze them! The focus is on your understanding of what the other person has to say rather than putting across your own views.

- When you are in agreement, openly say so; likewise give reasons why you might disagree with something. To have rapport you don't have to agree on everything, you just need to demonstrate empathy and show that you value the other person's views.

Matching

When you see people who have a natural rapport, there will be certain things you notice about them, for example energy levels in conversation, similarities in physiology and tone of voice, a synchronicity that shows both parties are in tune with each other. According to neurolinguistic programming (NLP) theory rapport can be enhanced by 'matching' your companion to generate a comfortable environment in which the other person feels their views will be understood. Matching is built on the close observation of others in order to match your behaviour to theirs by deliberately emulating some of their patterns. This is based on the simple premise that we like people who are like us and, the more evident this similarity, the easier it will be to develop the trust that is required when we have rapport.

Matching involves observing the other person to see how they hold their bodies, use gestures, facial expressions and so on. We can also listen for tonality, speech rhythm and particular words. One thing to be aware of is that matching is not mimicking; be careful not to copy all behaviours obviously because this might give the impression that you are making fun of the person, or trying to manipulate them. It is useful to use discretion and pause before you attempt to match anything to ensure that the conversation remains natural. Matching can also be achieved in a less direct way by using 'crossover matching', which involves choosing to match one of your behaviours to a corresponding but different behaviour in the other person, for example by changing the pace of your speaking to match the breathing patterns of the other, or tapping at the same pace as the other person's speech.

It is also possible to match language patterns by listening out for repetitive phrasing and acknowledging these by including some in your own contributions. In NLP, the term 'verbal predicates' is used to describe the ways in which an individual uses language to indicate how they process information from the world, and is based on the generalisation that we have a favoured way of representing the information we receive through our senses. Based on this hypothesis the language we use is said to be an indicator of our preferred way of making sense of the world, so, if we were an 'auditory' person, we might use phrases like 'I hear what you are saying' whereas someone who is more 'visual' might use the phrase 'I see what you mean'. Although there may be some merit in this in terms of creating similar communication patterns, it might also be a little simplistic, in that it doesn't take into account a range of other factors that may influence language use such as social and cultural conditioning, education and professional contexts.

The benefits of rapport in any relationship cannot be denied and it is certainly true that mentoring based on trust, empathy and congruence will be more successful than when it is based on other factors. As with many things, rapport is something that should, where possible, develop naturally to allow individual and mutual relationships to evolve in ways that allow both parties to have some agency rather than one dominating the other in order to get their own needs met.

How much rapport?

It is important to think about the amount of rapport you need to develop with your mentee. Although the aim is to create a supportive bond, there are also boundaries within this and too much rapport could be just as difficult as too little. If you consider levels of rapport as temperature points between 'hot' and 'cold', where would you consider the appropriate levels of rapport to be (Figure 2.1)?

Clearly either end of this scale has the potential to cross boundaries and, although some people may be comfortable operating at levels considered 'cosily warm' or 'cool' within professional contexts, the 'safe' approach would be to work towards overall acceptance.

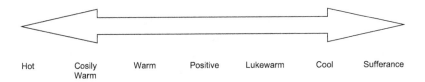

| Hot | Cosily Warm | Warm | Positive | Lukewarm | Cool | Sufferance |

Figure 2.1 Rapport temperature gauge

Unconditional positive regard

Any communication will be enhanced if it is conducted in a framework of mutual respect. Within many one-to-one settings this may be encapsulated by what Rogers (1961) refers to as 'unconditional positive regard', a phrase often employed within client-centred therapies. Although it is unrealistic to assume that we hold everyone we meet in high esteem, it is possible to respect everyone as a human being with the ability to make their own choices. Unconditional positive regard is based on the humanistic principles that people are inherently good and seek personal growth and self-fulfilment. Rogers believed that, to allow this to happen, it was important to show acceptance and support without questioning past or present behaviours, and to accept that each individual has the capacity to make their own choices.

Demonstrating unconditional positive regard is dependent on developing a relationship of trust and creating a 'safe' place for discussion free of judgement. This can be achieved by:

* Encouraging reflection
* Sharing thoughts and feelings about specific events
* Considering events from a range of perspectives
* Showing acceptance of another's views
* Showing empathy
* Avoiding judgements.

The consequence of this is that the other person feels free to experiment, to make and discuss mistakes and to learn from those experiences.

Setting up a contract

When you enter into a mentoring or coaching agreement it is easy to assume that the relationship will thrive on the sort of informality that exists between friends or close colleagues. Certainly, you will be working closely with your mentee and will be working hard at building rapport with them, as well as establishing a context in which unconditional positive regard is apparent; however, this does not mean that there will be no boundaries in place. After spending time creating the right climate for mentoring and building a bond based on trust, it might seem strange to discuss the more formal aspects of contracting. However, as with many other supportive associations, a contract provides a framework that ensures that all parties are clear on the expectations and limitations of their individual roles. This is not at all unusual in helping relationships; teachers will set ground rules with their class and therapists outline contracts with their clients. These are intended to provide structure and, by agreeing roles and expectations at the outset, you should ensure that the mentoring process supports its intended purpose.

In essence, your mentoring contract is an agreement about how you and your mentee will work together and, as such, is something you should draw up together. Although this will be a combined effort, it does make sense for the mentor to take charge of this stage initially by opening a discussion about the importance of contracting. An effective way of doing this would be to introduce some 'what-if' questions. – which will provide a starting point for the discussion.

> Think about the core values you listed in Chapter 1 and consider these in relation to your professional role. Now imagine you are working with a mentee who does a number of things to challenge those values, for example they were dishonest or did something that made you question their professionalism. Use this information to compile a series of 'what-if' questions.

Expectations and responsibilities

If we consider some of the definitions of mentoring explored in Chapter 1 it is quite difficult to identify what specific expectations mentors and mentees might have of the mentoring process, for example:

'A mentor is a person who helps another to think things through' (Pask 2004, cited in Pask and Joy 2007:8), in order to encourage autonomous learning, develop skills and maximise potential. Ultimately, it is about helping an individual to be the person they want to be.

In each of the previous examples the actual role of the mentor is not transparent; therefore, a mentee may not be entirely clear about what to expect. Other definitions of mentoring make reference to a supportive relationship, a teaching and learning relationship, and a reflective process whereas others refer to a vehicle for career development and a more formalised process. The fluidity of these definitions is appealing in that it suggests a certain flexibility, which may meet the needs of participants, but fluid definitions also create initial difficulties in outlining expectations.

> Jozefa had just started a teacher training programme and was very excited by the prospect of being allocated a mentor to support him through the course. Jozefa was confident that he would manage the practical side of teaching as he had some experience of working with groups of young people. He was less confident about his ability to write academic essays – or to complete any of the paperwork he knew he would have to do as part of the process, but he didn't need to worry because now he had a mentor to help him with that and he was determined to make the most of the opportunity. He was also feeling a little smug about how well organised he was and, in preparation for the first meeting with his mentor, Jozefa had drafted his first essay and put together skeleton lesson plans for his first week of teaching. He was hoping that he could leave these with his mentor to fine tune so that he could collect them the next time they met.

Jozefa's expectations of the support his mentor could provide could very well be different to his mentor's expectations, yet it could be encapsulated in the phrase 'support and encourage people to manage their own learning'. In this scenario, a meeting to establish what exactly the mentor and mentee would be bringing to the relationship would have been very useful in establishing a more positive and productive start.

The mentoring agreement

There are a number of things that need to be considered in a mentoring agreement and, although this is something that will vary according to individuals and specific contexts, Table 2.1 outlines some key considerations.

It may also be worth considering the emotional elements that may have an impact on the effectiveness of mentoring, for example are there any behaviours that may sabotage this, such as the mentor controlling all activities or the mentee being unresponsive to feedback? Similarly, are there any specific behaviours that will help the process, for example establishing a way of providing/using feedback in ways that will support progress?

Establishing an agreement at the outset will allow you to discuss and agree the practical, contextual and specific roles of the mentoring

Table 2.1 Things to consider in the mentoring agreement

Practical	Context	Roles
When will meetings take place? How long will they be? How will confidentiality be maintained? In what circumstances might confidentiality be broken? How will progress be measured? Are there any success criteria? Is there any paperwork to complete?	What is the purpose of mentoring in this context? Are there any professional guidelines/standards to consider? Are there any specific requirements as a result of the context? Is there a need to measure impact?	What will the mentor do? What will the mentee do? What are the boundaries of the mentoring relationship? How will mentor autonomy be maintained?

process, and ensure that each party's expectations are clarified before mentoring begins. It is also worth remembering that a mentoring agreement is not written on a tablet of stone and can be reviewed and amended periodically.

Mentee agency

Mentoring often involves working with mentees who are new to an organisation or a profession, and as such are not yet familiar with the structures that drive and control behaviours within that context. In this way mentoring can be viewed as a guiding role which helps the mentee to settle into the established norms and accepted practice. This can be a difficult element of the role to manage because it is also part of the mentor's remit to encourage the mentee to have agency, to ensure that mentees develop the capacity to make their own choices during and after the end of the mentoring relationship. As suggested by Rogers (1961), this forms part of providing unconditional positive regard in respecting the mentee's ability to 'Critically shape their responses to problematic situations' (Biesta and Tedder 2006:11).

When considering the terms of the mentoring agreement it is useful to discuss the concept of agency in order to establish what this means to your mentee. This will provide a forum from which you can ascertain the best ways to work together to ensure that the mentee is supported but not controlled by the mentoring process.

A sprinkling of magic

Creating the right environment for mentoring is essential in cultivating the trust that allows for open and honest communication. This in turn nurtures the reflective process, which is key in the critical evaluation of practice and advancement. In the same way that trees sometimes grow together yet remain independent, the mentor–mentee relationship evolves, each party taking different twists and turns, yet remaining in harmony.

Figure 2.2 A sprinkling of magic: trees in rapport

This chapter has outlined the ways mentors create positive, nurturing environments based on trust, empathy and congruence, through which mentees are empowered to accept their current 'story' and take ownership of their development. The development of harmonious relationships provides the opportunity for individuals to work together to achieve positive change in skills or perspective, a process that could be described as transformative (Mezirow 1997). This is not achieved by the casting of spells or the creation of magical elixirs but by recognising the elements that exist at individual and relational levels. Its magic lies in the opportunity for both mentors and mentees to change as a result of sharing perspectives, ideas, expertise and new learning.

Suggested further reading

Stewart, I. and Joines, V. (2003) *TA Today, a New Introduction to Transactional Analysis*. Nottingham and Chapel Hill: Lifespace Publishing.

References

Biesta, G. J. J. and Tedder, M. (2006). *How is Agency Possible? Towards an Ecological Understanding of Agency-as-achievement* (Working Paper 5). Exeter: The Learning Lives Project.

Erikson, E. H. (1994) *Identity: Youth and Crisis (No. 7)*. London: WW Norton & Co.

Lancer, N., Clutterbuck, D. and Megginson, D. (2016) *Techniques for Coaching and Mentoring* (2nd edn). Oxon: Routledge.

Lave, J. (1988) *Cognition in Practice: Mind, Mathematics, and Culture in Everyday Life*. Cambridge: Cambridge University Press.

Lave, J. and Wenger, E. (1991) *Situated Learning: Legitimate Peripheral Participation*. Cambridge: Cambridge University Press.

McAdams, D. P. (1985) *Power, Intimacy and the Life Story: Personological Inquiries into Identity*. Homewood, IL: Dorsey Press.

McAdams, D. and McClean, K. (2013) Narrative Identity. *Current Directions in Psychological Science*, 22(3): 233–238.

Mezirow, J. (1997) Transformative Learning: Theory to Practice. *New Directions for Adult and Continuing Education*, 74: 5–12.

Pask, R. and Joy, B. (2007) *Mentoring–Coaching a Guide for Education Professionals*. London: Open University Press.

Rogers, C. R. (1961) *On Becoming a Person: A Psychotherapist's View of Psychotherapy*. London: Constable & Robinson Ltd.

Stewart, I. and Joines, V. (2003) *TA Today, a New Introduction to Transactional Analysis*. Nottingham and Chapel Hill: Lifespace Publishing.

Wenger, E. (n.d.). Communities of Practice: A Brief Introduction. Available at: www.ewenger.com/theory/communities_of_practice_intro.htm [date accessed 10 August 2018].Excerpted with permission from Wenger, E.

Recognising boundaries

How do you look after the trees in your garden? Do you allow them to ramble and roam in any direction – or do you prune gently to maintain a boundary with the rest of the space? Pruning trees can make them safer – it enables them to live harmoniously within their environment; it may also increase their potential to bloom.

In this chapter, we explore the importance of boundaries and ethical practice within the mentoring relationship. In this case boundaries refer to the guidelines, the limits and the standards expected by both parties. In mentoring, such boundaries help everyone to understand the expectations of their own role and provide the security required to create a safe context in which to work.

Barriers in mentoring relationships

There are a number of potential barriers to effective mentoring which may influence the judgement of both parties. Some of these barriers relate to misconceptions held about the mentoring process, for example mentors must be seen as experts, mentors must be perfect and, linked to both of these, mentors are usually old! If mentoring starts out on the basis of such misconceptions, its value may be diminished.

Despite the espoused ideals of many organisations, mentoring is less prevalent in the workplace than we might expect and as a result the architecture required to support an organisation-wide mentoring pro-gramme may not be established. This means that participants don't necessarily know what to do, or how to 'be' in the mentoring process. This alone highlights the importance of communicating expectations from the outset but there are many other reasons for doing so, including openness, honesty and opening up a dialogue about the roles each of us has to play.

Where a programme is well established, this may also create a barrier. In this case, participation in a mentoring programme may be an expectation rather than a desire; therefore being a mentor or mentee becomes an obligation, or a mandate, rather than a choice. It is also possible that a formalised mentoring programme may have specific outcomes for mentees to achieve, together with the expec-tation that mentors help 'deliver' these outcomes through the support they provide. This has the result of changing the focus of the relationship from one that is based on development, normally led by the mentee's needs, to one that is underpinned by the organisation's need to evidence the effectiveness of mentor support. Although there is some value in aligning a mentoring programme to overall objectives, it is important that it isn't simply a tool for achieving key performance indicators because this will diminish its developmental impact.

Additional barriers exist in the form of external demands on individuals and the pressures associated with these. This has the potential to create anxiety about finding time for mentor–mentee meetings, which may not be deemed a priority when situated within the day-to-day workload.

Barriers to mentoring exist for both the mentor and the mentee, and it is important to recognise their potential for damaging the process and its impact. Typical barriers could be classified as those that are extrinsic or intrinsic. For example, environmental factors, work or home constraints and conflicting responsibilities are exter-nal to the individual and therefore represent extrinsic pressures. In addition, there are barriers that are intrinsically important such as motivation towards mentoring or self-efficacy of the mentor or mentee.

Using the headings 'intrinsic' and 'extrinsic' as a guide, create a list of the potential barriers you may have in relation to mentoring. Then repeat the process to outline some of the barriers that might be present for your mentee.

Power in professional relationships

Within many coaching and mentoring relationships, the pairing evolves out of one person's need to be guided by, or share the expertise of, another. This need immediately creates a power imbalance between participants because the 'more knowledgeable' person is seen as being more powerful than the novice. On the surface, this seems like a very natural occurrence and one with which most of us are familiar. Just think about all the relationships in life where the base of power is uneven: teacher and students, supervisor and trainee, manager and subordinate, employer and employee. This could extend to more personal relationships such as parent and child, husband and wife – or even most loved and least loved. Notions of power are embedded into our culture and may be generated in a number of ways, often based on what is deemed socially or culturally important. If you listed the things that may give one person perceived power over another, your list might include things such as age, gender, height, weight, wealth, position, social class and race. This may even be considered a positive by some because it creates a structure within which we may operate. In *The Republic*, Plato portrayed his ideas about the ideal society in which a 'guardian class' would organise matters of state, whereas others (slaves, workers, artisans) would be educated to understand their place within society. This was based on his view that economic power should be divorced from political power and that democracy should be replaced with government by those considered to have wisdom. This might seem a rather extreme scenario that does not meet with modern sensibilities or notions of democracy; indeed it was a reaction against the 'democracy' of the time, but it could be argued that a number of structures within modern society still serve this model.

In addition, Plato's views on the process of education might be considered to be similar to modern-day values in that the emphasis was placed on guiding those we teach through the 'Socratic method', an approach based on dialogue and the belief that learning is the result of questioning rather than telling. There was also clear recognition of the responsibility towards students, to seek out 'truth' and to support others in finding their own answers; a situation not dissimilar to that found in coaching and mentoring contexts.

When you begin a mentoring relationship, there will most likely be an imbalance of power, in that your mentee will look to you as the more knowledgeable other, to structure and guide the process. Therefore, as discussed in Chapter 2, it is the mentor's responsibility to find ways of working together, and alongside this consider the boundaries that should frame the way you work. It is important to remember that initially a power imbalance will have an impact on the ways in which you and your mentee communicate, so establishing ways of overcoming these barriers is an essential step in the process.

Boundaries

A mentoring relationship is based on open and honest communication and trust, so it seems strange to suggest that it also needs to have boundaries. Surely this would constrain communication and, as a result, limit development? This is a reasonable assumption but it is possible that clarity in relation to boundaries is something that helps everyone to understand the extent of the relationship and creates the freedom to explore within this. The very fact of their existence may actually enhance communication. If you consider other relationships within which you have open and honest communication, would you say they are boundary free? Do you feel comfortable talking about ANY topic? Are you at ease with whatever the other person wants to bring to the conversation? Take personal relationships, for example you may want to encourage complete openness with your partner but would this openness extend to sharing what you find attractive about another person in your life? Or discussing other relationships in which you found particular fulfilment? For most of us there are likely to be some emotional and cultural boundaries present within our relationships and yet we can still develop close and meaningful connections with others.

Patricia was finding her new role challenging but was thrilled to have a mentor with whom she could share things. Just having the space to explore her feelings and articulate her fears was a revelation to her, she had never really felt listened to before and the time with her mentor really made her feel valued as an individual. In the first few meetings Patricia was cautious about what information she shared but she soon learnt that her mentor was not judgemental and realised she could talk to her about anything. Even though this support was part of her new management role, Patricia felt that it would be useful to talk about some events in her past and at the last meeting she had done just that. In fact, she felt she had benefited so much from the conversation she had emailed her mentor to ask if they could meet up at the weekend to continue the discussion.

In this scenario, is there a possibility that Patricia and her mentor might have different ideas about the purpose of mentoring? As a mentor, would there be boundaries in relation to your personal time, or would you consider it appropriate to meet at the weekend? Mentoring relationships are not static and it is likely that the process opens up avenues that were not envisaged in the initial stages; the relationship ebbs and flows along its natural course but must still remain on some sort of course. In the case study, the issues from the past are not revealed but it is feasible that they are not related to the job role, which is the basis of your mentoring relationship, so you need to consider whether or not this is appropriate within your mentor agreement. It is also possible that the issues discussed need to be explored in a therapeutic context and if so are beyond the scope of the mentor's role and expertise.

In Chapter 2 we explored the practical aspects of setting up a mentoring agreement that should also take into consideration setting out expectations and boundaries. Some questions to consider are:

- What is the purpose of the mentoring relationship?
- In what ways can support be provided?
- What are the limitations to support?
- Is the relationship time-bound? Does it have a fixed start and end point?
- Will there be a specific format for meetings with an agreed day and time?
- Can both parties ensure a commitment to what has been agreed?
- Does the relationship fit within other organisational guidelines?
- How does the relationship support autonomy and independent thought?

Boundaries are simply guidelines that allow mentors and mentees to be comfortable with the extent of the relationship. They reinforce the purpose of the process and recognise its limitations as well as acknowledging that additional expertise may be required should the need arise.

Referring on

One boundary that most mentors will encounter is to acknowledge when additional, or alternative, support might be required. Although many coaching and mentoring models draw from therapeutic disciplines such as cognitive–behavioural therapy or transactional analysis, mentors do not usually undergo the training necessary to act as therapists in these disciplines and, as a result, do not have the skills required to support individuals with psychological issues. Although it is perfectly feasible that a mentor may also be a trained counsellor or therapist, it is worth remembering that this particular relationship was based on coaching or mentoring and usually for a specific purpose. It is not based on a client–therapist relationship, which is likely to involve exploring deeper issues. So, even if the mentor possesses the credentials to provide such support, doing so would be stretching the boundaries of the mentoring agreement.

A particular concern for many mentors is knowing when to refer mentees to other sources of support and when to try to address issues within the coaching or mentoring framework. Consider the following scenarios and make a decision as to whether you think these are situations that you could work with, or whether you would be more comfortable referring them on.

Barbara

Barbara is a trainee teacher who is undertaking her qualification as a mature student. She has been a little unreliable about her commitment to mentor meetings, often turning up quite late, or not at all. This has made it difficult to get to know her and it has been a struggle to create a rapport because she tends to be unresponsive to questioning, offering very little information about herself. She also seems to suffer from mood swings, is fidgety and can be quite snappy during meetings. Added to this, the things that Barbara does say do not seem to be consistent and there is a sense that she is not always telling the truth. This has recently been backed up by information received from Barbara's tutor who has suggested that Barbara has a complicated home life and often exhibits erratic emotions within lectures and seminars. At your last meeting with Barbara you noticed a strong smell of alcohol and are beginning to wonder if there may be further issues to consider.

Adam

Adam is a management trainee who has just completed his Masters' degree. When your mentoring relationship began Adam was enthusiastic and responsive. He seemed to value the opportunity to work with you. He was very keen to learn new

---

things and to set and achieve specific goals. He seemed to be enjoying the challenge of his new role. During your last two meetings, Adam has been much quieter and somewhat subdued. He is non-committal in his responses to questions about progress and he often looks disengaged, rarely makes eye contact and seems distracted. He has also developed a strategy of side-stepping your questions and trying to turn the conversation into a joke rather than responding to what was asked.

According to Clutterbuck (n.d.) there are several things to look out for when deciding whether or not you should refer on a mentee. These include:

- A constant depressed mood
- Problems related to alcohol or drug abuse
- Difficulties in achieving goals or concentrating on tasks
- Signs of frequent anger and not being able to control emotions
- Exhibiting high levels of anxiety
- When the mentee/coachee reveals a traumatic event that they have not been able to deal with
- Patterns of destructive or dysfunctional behaviour (such as self-sabotage at work or within relationships)
- Difficulties in forming relationships
- Breakdown of relationships
- Frequent and severe mood swings
- Frequent panic attacks.

In the two case studies were there any characteristics that would suggest you may need to refer one or both of the mentees to further support? You are perhaps questioning whether Barbara has issues relating to alcohol dependency or whether Adam is suffering from anxiety or depression and whether or not you had judged either situation correctly. The reality is, you don't really know in either case, and it is important to broach the topic of further support with sensitivity so that this action does not damage the mentoring relationship.

You may also question whether or not you should give advice to your mentee. This can be a difficult decision for many mentors and the answer very often lies in the specific mentoring agreement, which will outline the purpose and boundaries of the mentoring relationship. Within a democratic model of mentoring importance is placed on the autonomy of the mentee and this raises questions about the validity of providing very specific advice, something that is particularly pertinent in situations where you are using assumption to make judgements on the story being presented. According to Connor and Pokora (2012) giving advice to mentees is something that should be handled with care. They suggest that a better approach would be to ask yourself some questions that will help guide your actions. These include whether or not you could express your concerns in a non-judgemental way or whether, instead, you could create an opportunity for the mentee to discover potential blind spots. A further suggestion is to share information from your own experience, because this provides a safe example that is emotionally removed from the mentee and allows the opportunity to explore options.

What are ethics?

In professional life questions relating to ethical practice are an essential consideration. This is particularly true in professions that involve working directly with individuals who have the potential to be vulnerable or significantly influenced by our actions. But, in this context, what does 'ethical' mean? As with many other professions ethics in mentoring are often closely linked to values, which according to Mcleod are defined as 'an enduring belief that a specific end-state or mode of conduct is preferable' (Mcleod 2003:386). Or, as we outlined in Chapter 1, values could also be described as guidelines for how we choose to conduct our lives. Rokeach (1973) distinguishes between 'instrumental' and 'terminal' values, the former being the means by which we might achieve desired end states such as wisdom or comfort, and the latter the states themselves. When we are working within an ethical framework, it is as important to consider both instrumental and terminal values to ensure that our professional conduct is in keeping with other professionals. The initial challenge may be in deciding which of our values influences our ethical judgement and day-to-day practice. For this reason, it is useful to adopt an ethical framework that will provide the general guidelines for ethical decision-making.

An ethical framework

Although written for the therapeutic helping professions, the framework adopted by the British Association for Counselling and Psychotherapy (BACP) is equally useful in the mentoring context. This framework is based on values, principles and moral qualities that are considered to form the basis of good practice. This includes respecting individuals, enhancing wellbeing and capabilities, improving the quality of relationships, appreciating the value of human experience, and enhancing the quality of professional knowledge and its application. Such values could equally underpin a mentoring agreement. Based on the underpinning values, a number of key principles outline the ethical framework:

- Being trustworthy: honouring the trust placed in the practitioner
- Autonomy: respect for the client's right to be self-governing
- Beneficence: a commitment to promoting the client's wellbeing
- Non-maleficence: a commitment to avoiding harm to the client
- Justice: the fair and impartial treatment of all clients and the provision of adequate services
- Self-respect: fostering the practitioner's self-knowledge, integrity and care for self (British Association for Counselling and Psychotherapy 2016).

Dennis has undertaken his first supervision role, working with a Masters' student at his university. He gets on very well with the student and is really enjoying this part of his role but has recently discovered something that concerns him. His student has decided to take an unusual approach to his dissertation, which Dennis knows will not be appreciated by the other tutors who will be involved in assessing the work. They are very traditional and quite critical of anything that does not fit the normal dissertation format.

His student would like to submit part of the dissertation as a poem, which she feels is a creative approach to the work; however, it is quite unusual and not outlined in the course guidance, so Dennis knows this is a risk. He has explained this potential risk to the student who is adamant that this is the right way forward and will not be persuaded to adopt a more traditional approach.

In this scenario, Dennis is showing respect for his student's autonomy but is also concerned that his colleagues may not respond well to this deviation from the norm. He has tried being direct with the student but is mindful that he must also show respect for his colleagues and cannot share examples of their disdain for difference. He is torn between being very direct in his guidance and explaining once again the risks that are involved with taking an innovative approach, which he is aware may still be ignored, or being supportive in helping his student to produce the best dissertation she can, in the way she wants to produce it. He is also aware that, if his student does not get the outcome she wants, there may be further repercussions in terms of his support being questioned.

The principle of beneficence means that Dennis must make it clear to his student the risk she is taking and that this may have an impact on the overall outcome she could expect. In the interests of self-respect and care for self, Dennis should also ensure that he keeps very clear paperwork in relation to the guidance provided during supervision. Ultimately, Dennis must respect the autonomy of his student but can do so in the full knowledge that he has taken the necessary steps to ensure that she is aware of the potential consequences of her actions.

Personal and moral qualities

Ethical guidelines, unless underpinned by law, simply provide a framework from which to make potentially difficult decisions about a course of action. Although it is likely that adhering to such a framework will support you in making the right decision most of the time, there will be occasions where this is more difficult and it is important that your own ethical framework is also underpinned by your personal and moral qualities. As outlined by the BACP (2016), there are a number of personal and moral qualities that practitioners should aspire to in order to support their professional practice. In Figure 3.1 I have adapted this to represent those that I consider important within the mentoring context but it is worth reflecting on what is important to you.

Care is essential in the mentoring relationship in order to be supportive of someone else's development, and *diligence* ensures the reliable application of your mentoring skills to help your mentee achieve their outcomes while at the same time helping them to improve their professional agency. The very nature of mentoring requires the ability to demonstrate *empathy*, without this you are unable to communicate your understanding of your mentee's perspective and support them to achieve their aims, rather than imposing your own, or those of another body such as an employer. This also demonstrates *respect* for your mentee. A democratic approach to mentoring values the mentor's development as much as that of the mentee and as a result *humility* is required to acknowledge your own weaknesses. *Sincerity* represents a commitment to genuineness and a desire to be honest and open within the relationship. Finally, although mentors are not expected to know everything, there is an expectation that they have the ability to use their *wisdom* and sound judgement to inform their practice.

Figure 3.1 Mentoring qualities

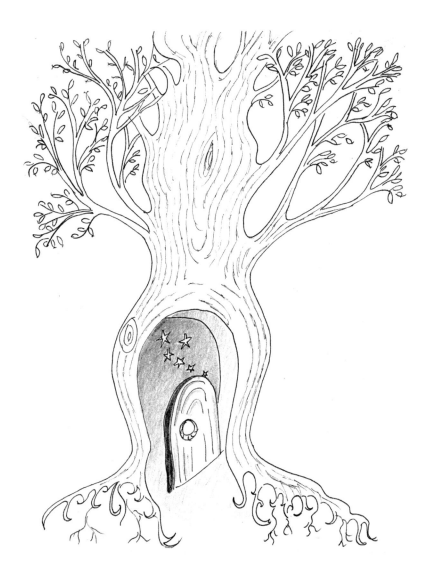

Figure 3.2 A sprinkling of magic: opening doors

A sprinkling of magic

The introduction of specific boundaries within a relationship might at first sight appear to constrain or limit possibilities, yet we could also argue that the boundaries themselves are the key to exploring potential. By creating a space in which we have agreed boundaries, we can communicate harmoniously, allowing the possibility of opening doors rather than closing them. In a sense, boundaries create the security to allow us to be ourselves, to reflect on our strengths and to consider possible developments.

Framing your mentoring practice within an ethical structure under-pinned by personal morals provides the foundations required for a relationship built on trust and mutual acceptance. This is a key principle for change and personal growth.

This chapter has considered the purpose of boundaries in mentoring and the importance of working within a strong ethical framework to provide both mentors and mentees with a safe space to explore ideas. In doing so it is possible to create the magic required for change to happen. According to a famous quote attributed to Goethe 'Magic is believing in yourself. If you can do that, you can make anything happen'.

Suggested further reading

British Association for Counselling and Psychotherapy. (2016) *Ethical Framework for the Counselling Professions*. London: BACP.

Clutterbuck, D. (n.d.) *When to Refer a Coachee or Mentee for Professional Counselling or Therapy*. Available at: https://coachingandmentoringinterna tional.org [date accessed 30 August 2017].

References

British Association for Counselling and Psychotherapy. (2016) *Ethical Framework for the Counselling Professions*. London: BACP.

Clutterbuck, D. (n.d.) *When to Refer a Coachee or Mentee for Professional Counselling or Therapy*. Available at: https://coachingandmentoringinterna tional.org [date accessed 30 August 2017].

Connor, M. and Pokora, J. (2012) *Coaching and Mentoring at Work, Developing Effective Practice* (2nd edn). Milton Keynes: Open University Press.

Goethe, J. W. (n.d.) Available at: https://www.goodreads.com/quotes/68691-magic-is-believing-in-yourself-if-you-can-do-that [date accessed 5 August 2018].

Mcleod, J. (2003) *An Introduction to Counselling* (3rd edn). Milton Keynes: Open University Press.

Plato. (1955) *The Republic*. London: Penguin. (Translated by H. P. D. Lee.)

Rokeach, M. (1973) *The Nature of Human Values*. New York: The Free Press.

Understanding ourselves and others

Do trees communicate in order to understand and support each other? Are they emotionally intelligent beings with heightened self-awareness and an empathy with their world? According to ecologists, plants have a far greater capacity to communicate with each other than is commonly believed. They do this through an information network made up of mycelia (vegetative structures in fungi) that create a sort of underground internet to connect the roots of different plants. This discovery has led to the development of 'plant neurobiology' which aims to investigate plant 'behaviours' such as memory, learning and problem solving (BBC Online).

In this chapter, we explore the importance of self-awareness in developing understanding of ourselves and others, and investigate the impact of emotions on behaviour and communication patterns. The chapter considers the concept of emotional intelligence and adopts a pragmatic approach to building emotional resilience through acknowledgement and acceptance of emotion within the mentoring context.

Emotional intelligence

The theory of emotional intelligence developed through studies of cognition and affect, more specifically looking at how emotions affect thoughts, and subsequently how thoughts influence behaviours. The term was originally created by Salovey and Mayer (1990) but was popularised by Daniel Goleman in his 1996 book, *Emotional Intelligence: Why It Can Matter More than IQ.* According to Salovey and Mayer, emotional intelligence represents an accurate appraisal of emotion in ourselves and others, and could be described as 'the subset of social intelligence that involves the ability to monitor one's own and others' feelings and emotions, to discriminate among them and to use this information to guide one's thinking and actions' (Salovey and Mayer 1990:190). Emotion in this view is regarded as something that organises our responses because of the way it allows us to focus cognitive attention and subsequent behaviours leading to actions.

An understanding of emotional intelligence (EI) provides a basis from which to identify and manage our own emotions, as well as those of others, skills that are essential in mentoring relationships. EI is generally considered to include three areas: emotional literacy, the ability to channel emotions, and application to thinking and problem solving. It also includes the skill of managing emotions, which means regulating your own emotions and positively influencing others: 'Being able to rein in emotional impulse; to read another's innermost feelings; to handle relationships smoothly' (Goleman 1996:xiii).

> So what does the emotionally intelligent person look like? Write a list of the skills and qualities you would expect to see in an emotionally intelligent mentor?

The development of skill in managing emotions is fundamental when working closely with others. When your role involves nurturing and guiding, it is even more important to be able to model the skills and qualities that will create empathetic relationships and enhance communication. In this type of relationship an emotionally intelligent person might display the following traits:

- Be in touch with their emotions
- Be able to control emotions sufficiently when communicating with others

- Be able to express emotions in appropriate ways
- Be able to deal with conflict
- Be able to demonstrate integrity and engender trust from others
- Be flexible in their approach to other people and to life
- Be able to cope with change
- Be realistic about their own strengths and weaknesses
- Be able to give constructive feedback to others
- Be able to learn from mistakes (McBride and Maitland 2002).

Emotional literacy

Emotional literacy refers to our ability to express our feelings by acknowledging and naming specific emotions, as well as our capacity to actively listen to, and empathise with, others. This seems like a simple enough task but, when you live and work in a culture that does not openly encourage discussion of emotion, developing the skills to talk about feelings is not necessarily a natural process. Consider your own experiences when you were growing up at home, or maybe your experiences in the workplace: did your family ask you to identify how you felt about specific events in your day, or were you encouraged to 'deal with things', or to 'get on with it'? At work, does your boss ask you how you feel about particular aspects of, or problems in your role – or is the expectation that you take a solutions-focused approach? How many times might you start a conversation with the words 'I feel' without any justification, explanation or even blame? Consider the difference between the following sentences:

'I feel you criticize my performance.'
'I feel criticized.'

Both acknowledge the same emotion but only one does so by taking ownership of it and without issuing blame.

The aim of enhancing our emotional literacy is to help us specify and effectively communicate our feelings and in doing so create greater clarity for ourselves and others. To do this we need to learn how to identify and name feelings in clear and concise ways. One recommendation is to practise using simple three-word sentences, for example 'I feel hurt'; 'I feel scared' or 'I feel happy'.

By identifying and naming feelings in this way we begin to enhance self-awareness, which in turn allows us to think about our responses to specific events, rather than simply reacting to things in instinctual or familiar ways. This helps avoid what Goleman refers to as 'emotional hijacking'. This term is used to describe the way in which the amygdala (the part of the brain responsible for processing base emotions) bypasses the 'thinking' part of the brain (the neocortex). The neocortex is intelligent and analytical, it can reason or make nuanced judgements, but the amygdala reacts immediately, causing us to respond to situations in familiar, rehearsed ways, often triggering a fight-or-flight response. Simply put, this means that the thinking, logical part of the brain is hi-jacked by its less rational and more emotional sister.

Acknowledging and naming emotions is a useful skill to model within the mentoring role. It is likely that your mentees will experience a range of things as they learn to accommodate different aspects of their development and begin to explore new approaches. It is also something that helps to create a non-judgemental arena for clear and honest communication, after all we cannot find ways of changing how we feel until we can accurately acknowledge the feelings.

Within our culture, it is not the norm to discuss our emotions openly; in fact this may be considered inappropriate or even a sign of weakness. We learn at an early age to block what we are feeling or sometimes to absorb the feelings that other people may place on us. I recall in my own childhood being told that I was tired, usually when I was irritable or angry. Being tired was an acceptable state of affairs to my mother, irritability and anger were not. Therefore I learnt to use the word 'tired' when what I was feeling was something entirely different. This may seem like an innocent thing but as an adult this can also lead to regular minimisation of emotion as a way of dissolving or ignoring anger. This in turn downplays the importance of significant events and can lead to maintaining behaviours or relationships that have a negative impact on your life. After all, there was nothing to be angry about, your husband, friend, boss (etc.) didn't mean to do that – you were simply over-reacting because you were tired!

All of this can make it difficult not only to acknowledge feelings, but also actually to know what it is we do feel; so one of the first steps to becoming more emotionally intelligent is to recognise (and by default avoid dismissing) emotions. According to Brown (2015) this is the skill of 'reckoning with' our emotions, which simply put means recognising and acknowledging them, then getting curious about how we feel and how this connects to our behaviour. This sounds simple enough but if you have become skilled at ignoring your emotions, it may take some practice before you can accurately label them. Read the following reflection and try to pinpoint the feeling you might experience in this scenario.

You have spent the last six months working on a project which you have just completed. The process has been hard work and has consumed a lot of your personal time, but it has also been very rewarding. It is an area of your work that you feel very passionate about and something in which you have genuine expertise. One of your colleagues was also involved in the project but quite openly admitted to you that it wasn't really his area and he was happy for you to take the lead. This was something you did willingly and felt you worked well with your colleague by keeping him informed and taking into account his views and opinions. All in all, it has been a very positive experience.

The time has now come to share the project outcomes with the rest of your team. Your colleague has asked if he can lead on this because he would like to feel as if he has done his share of the work. As you don't want to hurt his feelings, and also acknowledge that he is a very charismatic presenter, you agree and offer to add detail where required. After all, you will still get your say and it might make the presentation run more smoothly.

When the presentation takes place your colleague dominates the event, leaving you little time to add your own thoughts and ideas. At the end, the team congratulate him on all the work he has done and your boss thanks him effusively – and then remembers to add your name as if it were an afterthought.

How did that scenario make you feel? What emotions were you initially aware of? Was it difficult to name specific emotions? Sometimes correctly acknowledging emotions can be complex because we are not used to using the actual words that represent them. How often do you express feelings such as resentment or hostility? Bliss or anguish? It is probable that many of the words we use to express emotion are not part of our day-to-day vocabulary and, if this is the case, Table 4.1, which lists common positive and negative emotions, may be useful.

Channelling and applying emotions

Emotions have a very practical purpose in our lives. If we consider core emotions such as love and fear, they have very definite roles: love may lead us to connect with others or to procreate and fear helps to keep us safe. However, emotions are also subject to interpretation and as a result may lead us to developing habitual behaviour patterns, which, although useful when originally adopted, no longer serve us in the way we would like. Consider the examples shown in Table 4.2.

The examples provided are intended to illustrate how early decisions can influence us in later life. All feelings are experienced at an individual level and the way that we make sense of them, as well as the decisions we make as a result of this analysis, are equally individual. For example, Lesley could just as easily respond to criticism by becoming a perfectionist and Marco may respond to his family's

Table 4.1 Positive and negative emotions

Positive emotions	Negative emotions
Bliss, compassion, confidence, connection, contentment, delight, excitement, euphoria, ecstasy, enthusiasm, freedom, gladness, gratitude, happiness, harmony, hope, inspiration, joy, merriment, motivation, optimism, passion, peace, safety, rapture	Apprehension, alarm, anguish, anxiety, bitterness, dejection, despondency, dismay, distress, dread, frustration, gloom, grief, irritation, melancholy, misery, nervousness, unhappiness, regret, resentment, remorse, sadness, stress, terror, trepidation, worry

Table 4.2 Examples of interpretations of emotions

The story	The decision	The outcome
Dan is told by his parents: 'Those who ask don't get.'	Dan decides not to ask for anything.	Dan feels misunderstood and that no-one really 'gets' him.
Katie's father is more affectionate towards her when she behaves in a 'girly' way.	Katie learns to adopt young and feminine mannerisms.	Katie feels she is often treated as a child and isn't taken very seriously at work.
Patricia's mother and her friends often talk about being let down by the men in their lives.	Patricia decides that men are not trustworthy.	Patricia struggles to commit to her partner.
John's mother always introduces him with the phrase: 'This is John – he makes us laugh.'	John learns that his role is to make others happy.	John feels uncomfortable getting what he wants and puts everyone else first.
Lesley's brother likes to laugh at her mistakes and makes fun of her.	Lesley becomes afraid of making mistakes.	Lesley can be paralysed by the fear of criticism.
Marco's family often use the phrase 'look before you leap'.	Marco learns not to take risks.	Marco feels trapped in his life.

saying by becoming analytical and weighing up the pros and cons of specific actions. Emotions and actions are inextricably linked, but specific emotions do not have specific corresponding actions; they are analysed and interpreted at an individual level. As Burns states this has more to do with the messages we give ourselves about events than the events themselves. Burns (1989) stresses that, by learning to change our thoughts, we can also change the way we feel. The ability to acknowledge and name emotions and as Brown (2015) suggests, 'reckon with' them, is a first step towards building the emotional resilience required for anyone working in helping roles.

According to Grant and Kinman (2013) emotional resilience might be described as the ability to recover from adversity, to 'bounce back' when things become difficult; they stress the importance of using appropriate strategies to do so. Their literature review highlighted a range of attributes associated with such resilience within the helping professions, these included:

- Self-awareness
- Self-efficacy
- EI/literacy
- Reflective ability
- Optimism
- Social confidence
- Sense of humour
- Accurate empathy
- Good support networks
- Effective coping skills
- Commitment to self-care
- Problem-solving skills
- Cultural competence
- A commitment to professional values
- Work–life balance.

If emotional resilience includes things like self-awareness, the ability to be reflective, and a sense of humour and optimism, it might seem that these are simply personality traits, but there is evidence to suggest they are skills we can all develop if we cultivate a belief in our own ability to do so.

The term 'self-efficacy' can be defined as a person's beliefs about their capability to exercise influence over events that affect their lives. The term was developed by Albert Bandura (1977) as part of social cognitive theory which acknowledges the role of cognition and motivation in directing our behaviours. According to Bandura, what people think, believe and feel affects how they behave and has an impact on how we motivate ourselves to achieve desired outcomes. Bandura described self-efficacy as being part of the 'self-system' which has a significant influence on how we perceive and respond to a range of situations, as well as our ability to direct action that helps us to achieve the outcomes we want. All individuals can identify things they want to change but how they approach these challenges will differ. Individuals with a strong sense of self-efficacy tend to view challenges as problems to be mastered, whereas those with a weak sense of self-efficacy will believe that these things are beyond their capabilities and as a result may avoid difficult tasks. An example of some initial differences in approach can include a person with a strong sense of self-efficacy who may:

- See problems as challenges
- Develop an intrinsic interest in activities
- Form a stronger sense of commitment to their interests and activities
- Recover quickly from setbacks and disappointments
- Sustain efforts in the face of failure.

On the other hand, someone with a weaker sense of self-efficacy may:

- Avoid challenging tasks
- Have lower aspirations
- Have less commitment to goals
- Believe that difficult tasks and situations are beyond their capabilities
- Focus on personal failings and negative outcomes
- Lose confidence in personal abilities.

Consider the story of two little boys at the seaside. Is the second little boy an example of a child who will develop a strong sense of self-efficacy? What messages must have been provided and digested for his current self-belief?

Two little boys

A teacher was sitting on the wall resting after a long hike on the Cornish coastal path. She was eating a sandwich and observing events on the beach. Two young boys, around six years old, were playing together. They'd been running around for a while, having fun and now, a little tired from their activities, they sat down near her and began talking.

Perhaps they had just met as children easily do on holiday; at any rate they seemed to have a lot to talk about. Finally, one said to the other 'What do you want to be when you grow up? I'm going to be a brain surgeon.'

Gosh I don't really know. I've never thought about it. I'm not very bright you know.

The Cornish wind took the rest of their conversation away and the teacher was left wondering where that second little boy developed his limiting belief about himself. Probably from another teacher! Or a parent. At the age of six, if he doesn't change that belief, or if someone else doesn't help him to change it, it will affect the rest of his life, limiting his sense of possibility, holding back his potential.

Beliefs are not true. They are constructs around which we organise our behaviours. So we each behave as if our beliefs were true, and for this reason all our beliefs come true, for beliefs, whether empowering or limiting, are self-fulfilling prophecies (Owen 2001).

Bandura believed that we are influenced by 'verbal persuasion' from significant people in our lives (such as parents, teachers and managers) and these experiences can strengthen or weaken our beliefs in our ability to succeed. In time, those messages are introjected through our process of internal communication; in effect, our brain believes and accepts the messages we are conveying to it. So, telling ourselves we can, or can't, do something is a powerful factor in developing self-efficacy.

Verbal persuasion from others can also be a useful tool in helping to develop confidence and is something that can be embedded within the mentoring role. When mentors provide constructive feedback, alongside verbal confirmation of their belief in the mentee's ability, this can be very powerful in enhancing development. Similarly, the use of vicarious experience can be beneficial in helping mentee's to develop specific skills or behaviours. Observing someone else perform a task, or handle a particular situation, will show how this activity can be conducted successfully and will provide a framework from which mentees can develop their own approaches.

It is important to remember that we are not born with a level of self-efficacy that we maintain throughout our lives. Developing a strong sense of self-efficacy is something we can cultivate with practice and we become more emotionally resilient as we learn to do this. Think of it as a continuum where you might start with a weak sense of self-efficacy but, through practising different ways of thinking and approaching tasks, move through the continuum until you achieve the outcome you want.

So how do we learn to develop our self-efficacy sufficiently to provide the ability to 'bounce back' from adversity and are there any specific strategies we can employ to help our mentees do this? Burns (1989) suggests an approach referred to as the 'four steps to happiness'. This is based on a model of reflection and analysis which highlights automatic thoughts as well as distortions in thinking. In practice this would work by following these four steps:

1. Identifying the situation
2. Recording your negative feelings about the situation
3. Using the triple-column technique to tune into automatic thoughts, feelings and distortions
4. Then reviewing how much you believe in the automatic thoughts originally specified.

It is a step-by-step approach to enhancing objectivity into our thinking by removing ourselves from the initial thoughts and emotions. The triple-column technique involves creating a table to include the areas outlined in Figure 4.1.

An example of how this might work in practice is shown in Table 4.3.

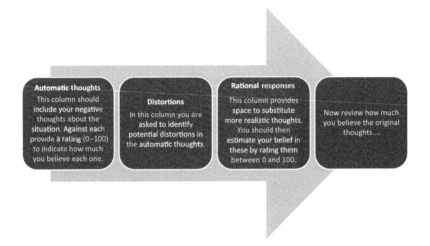

Figure 4.1 The triple-column technique

Table 4.3 Using the triple-column technique

Automatic thoughts	*Distortions*	*Rational responses*
I didn't express myself clearly today and my presentation was a disaster. (80) The audience was bored. (80) They must think I don't know what I am talking about. (80)	Was it a disaster? Did you get through it? Did people walk out? The audience was quiet but they did answer questions when asked. Are the audience experts in the field? How do you know what they are thinking?	My presentation was not as good as it could have been because I was nervous. (100) Some of the audience may have been bored but some people were engaged.(90) I don't know what the audience thinks so there is no point in mind reading. I do know my stuff. (90)

Knowing ourselves

An important aspect of enhancing emotional resilience is increasing our self-awareness, as highlighted by the well-known quote attributed to Socrates: 'To know thyself is the beginning of wisdom.' There are of course many things we know about ourselves that are integrated into day-to-day life, for example most of us know our name, our age, our sexual preferences; it is questionable whether or not this knowledge makes us any 'wiser'. However, self- knowledge may also include aspects of ourselves that are less overt, possibly things we find more difficult to accept, for instance we may know that we are more selfish than we would like to admit, that we are not as daring as we would love to be or that we don't really like children or animals. So what does it mean to know yourself in a way that is useful to your personal and professional development?

In this context, to know ourselves means to be able to view ourselves objectively. According to Brown (2012) this is about practising authenticity as well as opening up to vulnerability.

Within the mentoring relationship, this is something that can be developed through the creation of rapport and the growth of trust. As outlined in Chapter 2, creating an environment in which open communication is encouraged enhances our ability to reflect objectively and without judgement, thereby providing a first step towards challenging assumptions and beliefs we have previously accepted about ourselves.

Johari's window

An interesting technique for helping to improve self-knowledge is Johari's window which presents a model based around four quadrants to represent aspects of the personality (Luft and Ingham 1955). A simple adaptation of this model is shown in Figure 4.2.

The model was originally based on the premise that self-disclosure and feedback were useful in helping individuals to understand more about themselves through communicating and building trust with

Figure 4.2 Johari's window

others. It may be considered a heuristic technique, in that it is not a perfect tool for self-discovery, but within the mentoring context it does provide a starting point for discussion; for this reason it may be a very useful technique for structuring a mentoring meeting.

In this model, the open area provides a non-threatening start because this is based on things that are in the public domain, and might include specific skills and abilities that have already been demonstrated. The blind area represents aspects of self that could be considered 'blind spots', things that others may be aware of but the individual is not. Blind spots are particularly important within the mentoring relationship because these provide opportunities to raise questions and give feedback on specific aspects of performance or behaviour; as such they are a stepping stone to further development. It is possible that your mentee is displaying a particular behaviour that is limiting their progress, for example you may have noticed that your mentee always interjects with ideas and answers, without really listening to what others are saying. Although this may indicate enthusiasm and a willingness to participate, it also detracts from the potential to learn from an interaction because continued talking means they are not focused on listening and could be missing out on important information.

The hidden area represents things that we know about ourselves but others do not know. These may be aspects of our personality or our work performance that we are not ready to share, perhaps because they are things we are not proud of, or maybe because we fear disapproval or rejection. There may be very valid reasons why some information in this quadrant is not openly shared and it is beyond the scope of the mentoring relationship to delve too deeply into this. It is natural for private and personal information to remain hidden and much of this will have no bearing on the mentee's role, so it can and should remain undisclosed. However, other information in this quadrant may not be very personal and may simply be hidden because the mentee requires 'permission' to disclose it, for example a mentee who is new to a particular role may be well aware that there are aspects of their role they are not particularly skilled at, but having just been appointed they are not yet ready to highlight this lack of expertise. These hidden aspects could be moved into the open area through a process of discussion and disclosure. There is also potential to explore hidden capabilities by encouraging your mentee to be open to trying new things and experiences.

The unknown area may contain a variety of things such as latent abilities, aptitudes or feelings, and they represent areas of discovery. Typically they might include things like underestimating skills and abilities because they have not been tested by experience, conditioned behaviours or attitudes from childhood. This information can be uncovered through self-discovery, reflection, observation and feedback from others and, sometimes, simply by trying out new things. All of these activities have the potential to provide opportunities for genuine, and potentially transformative, learning.

A sprinkling of magic

Being aware of and open to emotion is just as valid in the workplace as it is within our personal lives. The development of emotional literacy

Figure 4.3 A sprinkling of magic: emotional growth

within the mentoring relationship provides a forum from which to explore our strengths and limitations within a supportive framework. By becoming attentive to and accepting of our limitations, and vulnerability, we also create potential for growth.

This chapter has considered the notion of EI and introduced practical strategies for developing emotional resilience. For many mentors, this may not be a part of the role they had originally anticipated but, if we are to explore potential fully and encourage positive change, it is an important consideration. By being more open with ourselves and others, there is also a risk that we become more vulnerable, but this is taken alongside the prospective benefit of enhanced authenticity and, as suggested by the following quote, the rewards may outshine the pitfalls: 'the day came when the risk to remain tight in a bud was more painful than the risk it took to blossom'[1] (Anais Nin Blog 2013).

Note

1 This quote is often attributed to Anais Nin but has not been found in her work; it has been claimed by Elizabeth Appell.

Suggested further reading

Brown, B. (2015) *Rising Strong*. London: Vermilion.
Goleman, G. (1996) *Emotional Intelligence: Why It Can Matter More than IQ*. London: Bloomsbury.

References

Anais Nin Blog. (2013) Available at: http://anaisninblog.skybluepress.com/2013/03/who-wrote-risk-is-the-mystery-solved/ [date accessed 7 August 2018].
Bandura, A. (1977) Self-efficacy: Toward a Unifying Theory of Behavioural Change. *Psychological Review*, 84: 191–215.
BBC Online. Plants Can See, Hear and Smell – And Respond. Available at: www.bbc.com/earth/story/20170109-plants-can-see-hear-and-smell-and-respond [date accessed 5 January 2018].
Brown, B. (2012) *Daring Greatly: How the Courage to Be Vulnerable Transforms the Way We Live, Love, Parent, and Lead*. New York: Gotham.

Brown, B. (2015) *Rising Strong*. London: Vermilion.

Burns, D. D. (1989) *The Feeling Good Handbook*. New York: Penguin Books.

Goleman, G. (1996) *Emotional Intelligence: Why It Can Matter More than IQ*. London: Bloomsbury.

Grant, L. and Kinman, G. (2013) 'Bouncing Back?' Personal Representations of Resilience of Student and Experienced Social Workers. *Practice, Social Work in Action*, 25(5): 349–366.

Luft, J. and Ingham, H. (1955) The Johari Window, a Graphic Model of Interpersonal Awareness. *Proceedings of the Western Training Laboratory in Group Development*. Los Angeles, CA: University of California, Los Angeles.

McBride, P. and Maitland, S. (2002) *The EI Advantage, Putting Emotional Intelligence into Practice*. Maidenhead: McGraw-Hill.

Owen, N. (2001) *The Magic of Metaphor, 77 Stories for Teachers, Trainers and Thinkers*. Carmarthen: Crown House Publishing Ltd.

Salovey, P. and Mayer, J. D. (1990) Emotional Intelligence. *Imagination, Cognition, and Personality*, 9: 185–211.

Stenier, C. and Perry, P. (1997) *Achieving Emotional Literacy*. London: Bloomsbury.

Nurturing the mentoring relationship

A tree will not grow without sunshine or water. It needs air to breathe and space to branch out. If the environment is too controlled, too dark or too suffocating, it will not grow to its full potential; it may even wither and die. Take the Bonsai tree, for example; this is actually a normal tree but is kept small by aspects of its environment; it is grown in a small pot so has no room to expand and it is pruned significantly in order to make it neat and pleasing to the eye. But does the Bonsai reach its full potential as a healthy, nurtured tree?

In this chapter, we consider how to create an environment that nurtures the practical and emotional aspects of the mentoring relationship. We will also discuss the development of a pro-social culture through the use of non-judgemental communication and explore the importance of congruence in one-to-one interactions.

Creating a nurturing environment

Describing what constitutes a nurturing environment may not be as simple as it seems. We each have different needs in relation to what nurtures us and different perceptions about what might make us feel deprived. Although it is impossible to outline all of the individual factors that may cause us to feel supported or otherwise, there are two key considerations that have an impact on the creation of a nurturing environment for mentoring: the physical environment and the emotional climate.

The physical environment

There are some things that you will have little or no control over, such as the actual room allocated for mentor meetings, but small steps taken to create a welcoming environment will have a positive impact on your interaction with mentees. It is important to construct an atmosphere that fosters collaboration and if possible creates a sense of wellbeing. Some considerations are:

- Light: is there an area of natural light, or can lighting be altered so that it is not too harsh?
- Space: is there a comfortable space for both of you to sit, without obstructions such as large desks or cabinets? Some people believe that any furniture between both parties acts as a barrier but I have found things like a round table, where you can sit next to each other, works really well and provides space for taking notes or looking at things that may be a focus for the meeting.
- Privacy: can you make sure that you are not disturbed during your meeting? Or can you organise the room layout so that you have a private area in it? This is particularly important if you have to give some feedback to your mentee or if you want them to open up about something.
- Can you have a dedicated space for mentor meetings? If so, would it be appropriate for you to introduce colour and some interesting objects (art, plants, posters etc.).

Emotional climate

Constructing a healthy emotional climate in which the mentoring relationship can flourish requires attending to a number of factors. In Chapter 2, we explored the importance of building a rapport based on mutual attentiveness, positivity and the sense that there is a connection and both parties are 'in sync'. We also discussed Rogers' concept of unconditional positive regard, adopting a premise of acceptance of each other by removing judgement and increasing understanding. Other factors that will help generate a healthy emotional climate are the development of non-judgemental communication and the demonstration of empathy.

Non-judgemental communication

The main principle of non-judgemental communication is the avoidance of criticism and blame, both of which can make the other person defensive and closed. Being non-judgemental is also about being authentic, which means we need to demonstrate an awareness of our own judgements and how they might influence the ways we communicate with others. Making judgements is of course a natural process and something that probably evolved to keep us safe; we needed to judge others on the basis of whether or not they were a threat to us. However, making judgements and being judgemental should be viewed as quite different things. When we make judgements we try to do so by weighing up the evidence that is presented to us and making an evaluation of a given situation based on that evidence. Being judgemental usually refers to being overly critical, generally in an unhelpful way and, as outlined earlier, is associated with allocating blame often based on limited evidence. We are frequently judgemental in relation to quite superficial things, such as how people look, or speak, their lifestyle, their views. The key here is not to become a saint (see how easy it is – there is a judgement) but to be aware of your own prejudices, to try to understand them and be open to people presenting evidence that may prove you wrong.

Kevin is a trainee teacher who is on a placement in a secondary school. He is a bright and enthusiastic student who says he is passionate about teaching and works hard to make all of his lessons interesting. After working with Kevin for a while you notice that he seems quite critical of his colleagues, who he refers to as 'dinosaurs' while telling you that 'they are completely

> out of touch with pupils and cannot be bothered to change the way they do things'.

Is Kevin's statement a judgement or is he being judgemental? The lack of evidence presented about his 'prehistoric' colleagues suggests the latter and Kevin is clearly being judgemental about others without exploring the facts. An alternative approach might be for him to talk to his colleagues about how they structure their teaching and why they do things in particular ways. The likelihood is that years of experience have provided some insight into strategies that work; alternatively they may say they have simply chosen not to change things because it is too much trouble. But, without this information, Kevin's comments remain in the judgemental camp.

> Kerry has embarked on a management trainee programme and is discussing her options for undertaking a supported project within the organisation. She says she feels lucky to have been offered the choice of two options, both of which she thinks are exciting opportunities, but she is struggling to make her mind up about which one to select. After some thought, Kerry has decided to make her decision based on the colleagues she will be working closely with and she outlines her observations about each of them, as well as her thoughts on how each might help her to develop her own skills. Her comments are focused on the skills and traits she has recognised in both colleagues and how they match, or challenge, her own.

Is Kerry's approach judgemental? Or is she making a judgement? This example shows that Kerry has gone through a process of evaluation by isolating factors that might influence how she would work with each of her colleagues and, although these factors include personal traits, they are assessed in relation to how they might be compatible with her own. This has been done in an objective and non-judgemental way.

Psychological projection

It is probably safe to say that we are all judgemental at times and much of this tendency is based on the ways we have experienced and learned to interpret the events of our lives. Often, the things we are judgemental about fall into the categories of learned behaviours, including things we have explicitly been taught, and fears about 'hidden' aspects of ourselves. Psychological projection is the idea that we defend ourselves, or our accepted image of ourselves, by denying these hidden aspects of self while attributing them to others. For example, my sister constantly tells me things about my behaviour, often things about my very being, which seem to be a mirror image of her own behaviours, using statements such as 'You always think you know best', generally following a conversation where she tells me what to do or not do, or 'You are so intolerant' after she has explained how a certain group of people are one thing or another (insert your own choice from lazy, bad-mannered, untrustworthy). I too, am guilty of uttering my frustrations about colleagues who complain they never have time to research because their lives are so busy, while simultaneously moaning about my own list of chores and lack of progress! In his book about addiction, Gabor Maté describes this process succinctly:

> When I am sharply judgmental of any other person, it's because I sense or see reflected in them some aspect of myself that I don't want to acknowledge.
>
> (Maté 2009:254)

Projecting our own uncomfortable thoughts and emotions on to others is a way of considering them without feeling them at a visceral level, so we can criticise others and distance ourselves from our own discomfort. So why is this knowledge important to the mentoring role? If we are to work in an authentic way, recognising projection in ourselves and others is helpful in getting to what really concerns us and, although it isn't recommended that you forcefully challenge signs of projection, it is worth considering how it might be influencing the stories being presented. Using a reflective approach is helpful in diminishing projection; if we, or our mentees, are seeing others in a negative way, then we might want to consider if we are projecting. This can be done by using specific questions to elicit more information about a particular incident. For example, you could ask how a particular occurrence made them feel, or what specifically it was that bothered them about the incident/person. You could perhaps ask what assumptions they are making about the incident/person. Or maybe what they would have done differently.

Empathy

Empathy is something most of us probably feel we have even if we can't exactly define it. According to Daniel Goleman it relates to awareness of others, their feelings and their concerns. According to psychologists there are three types of empathy: cognitive empathy, emotional empathy and compassionate empathy.

As the name suggests, cognitive empathy has an analytical component; in a sense it is a 'perspective taking', which means you may be able to see another's perspective but will not necessarily feel it. This allows you to take a particular viewpoint without engaging with emotions and can be a very useful skill when you are trying to calm down a reaction to a specific event, while at the same time demonstrating a clear understanding of it.

Emotional empathy is established when you can feel what the other person is going through. This is sometimes referred to as emotional contagion, which describes the way we are able to absorb and mimic other people's emotions by picking up on small signals such as facial expressions, body language and change in voice tone. It could be described as a virus, as if the emotions themselves are floating around the room and infecting its inhabitants. According to Hatfield et al. (1994) this process is linked to our tendency to mimic the expressions of others and in doing so begin to feel some of what they are feeling. So by attending to these feelings in ourselves it is possible to 'feel ourselves' into the emotional terrain of others.

Empathy of course can lead to vicarious pain. If we are genuinely feeling what others are feeling and they are in pain, we must also feel pain. Compassionate empathy has a more pragmatic element. It could be described as feeling what others are feeling but at the same time being driven to help in more pragmatic ways. So, we feel concern for someone, through compassion, but also focus on providing support to mitigate any painful emotions.

Empathy is of course an important element of creating a nurturing environment in the mentoring context because it provides the ability to recognise and respond to whatever your mentee is experiencing. Without it we can appear insensitive; we may jump to conclusions based on our own experiences of similar situations and we may fail to understand the other person's needs. The use of compassionate empathy also provides a building block from which to explore possible solutions to issues and concerns, but how do we demonstrate empathy in ways that show genuine concern?

As outlined previously in this chapter, the demonstration of empathy requires the ability to communicate in non-judgemental ways. This means you may have to put aside your own viewpoint and validate the other person's perspective. This can be done by acknowledging what you are being told without making a judgement or trying to fix it. It also requires the ability to listen and to demonstrate that you have been listening.

One technique that can be used to good effect is reflecting back to the other person. This can be done to test understanding and to build on what you have been told. One common reflecting technique is mirroring which is a simple and almost exact repetition of what has been said. This does show the person that you have indeed listened, but is a technique that should be handled with care. Mirroring is intended to be short and simple, so you can just repeat the key phrase or a few words, rather than whole sentences. Be wary of over-using this strategy because it can come across as mechanistic if not followed by other approaches and can lead to nothing more than a circuitous route of the conversation.

It is important to convey a sense of genuine curiosity and this can be achieved by using clarifying questions to deepen your understanding of certain points, for example:

'When you said . . ., what did you mean?'
'Tell me more about . . .'

'What you seem to be saying is ...'

'I just want to make sure that I understand what you are saying by ...'

You can also use paraphrasing both to check your understanding of what you are being told and to convey that you are genuinely listening to, and trying to understand, the other person. In this case you need to restate what you have been told in simple terms without adding to the meaning, analysing or taking the topic in a new direction. The key to this is to focus on the main idea and try to avoid getting bogged down in detail.

Sue tells you about a meeting with her manager that she is clearly upset about:

She just doesn't listen, sometimes it is like addressing a brick wall. I know why, I am not one of her favourites so my opinion doesn't really count ... there are two or three people she really listens to and the rest of us have to find other routes for getting information to her. I tested this once by getting a colleague to put forward an idea of mine she had dismissed ... and guess what? It is so frustrating. I tried very carefully to explain why I couldn't change the schedule for the project but it fell on deaf ears. Honestly, she can be so rude sometimes. She just put forward her point of view then turned back to her computer and started typing! I now have a project with an unrealistic budget and I don't know how I will complete it. I need to talk to her again but feel so angry about the way she dismissed me.

How would you paraphrase Sue's story? Which elements of it are important and which provide additional detail? The key points seem to be: Sue is concerned that she cannot complete the project on the current budget. She feels her manager doesn't listen to her and has dismissed her concerns. At a practical level you may just select the first of these points, because, from a business perspective, that would be the focus, but it is clear from Sue's description that there is some emotion attached to feeling dismissed, so it is important to acknowledge that too if you want to demonstrate empathy.

Using these techniques for the first time can seem like a minefield and it is very easy to get caught up in judging your own performance as a listener, which in turn will take your attention away from focusing on your companion and demonstrating empathy! For this reason it is important not to judge yourself too harshly and remember that your mentee knows you are trying to help, so:

- Be yourself and keep it natural
- Relax and listen for the basic messages
- Observe other signals, such as expressions and gestures
- Use paraphrasing to restate what you have heard in simple terms
- Use questions to clarify meaning
- Avoid taking things in a different direction
- And, perhaps most important, remember that you are not expected to be perfect.

Developing a pro-social culture

Pro-social behaviours are those that are focused on helping other people. They could include things such as sharing, cooperating or volunteering, and underpin most mentoring relationships. They are in effect voluntary actions aimed at helping individuals and the community as a whole, and can be seen among humans, animals and even trees. Pro-social behaviour has been linked to altruism but reasons for behaving pro-socially, as opposed to anti-socially, may not always be altruistic. There are lots of positive outcomes for the 'helper' as well as the 'helped', including advancing knowledge and skills, having a sense of purpose, working with others and reciprocity; after all, when we help others, it is more likely that they will choose to help us should we need it. The mentoring relationship is a perfect example of the benefits of pro-social behaviour. Mentors, while helping others, also gain skills, confidence and knowledge from being involved in the relationship.

The relationship itself is based on philanthropic foundations and includes examples of many pro-social behaviours, such as supporting, listening and helping find solutions to problems. Another, perhaps natural aspect of mentoring is the mentor's role in building their mentee's confidence, through the use of praise and encouragement. Some simple ways of doing this are by highlighting what has gone well or picking out positive skills or traits your mentee is developing. You might also communicate your faith in your mentee's capacity to grow and reach their goals by offering words of encouragement.

The Pygmalion effect

The impact of encouragement can be taken a step further by not only communicating your faith in your mentee's abilities but also articulating your expectations of them. According to the work of Rosenthal and Jacobsen (1968), expectations influence performance. Rosenthal is well known for his experiments with students observing rat mazes. In these experiments students were asked to test rats who were labelled 'maze smart' or 'maze dull'; they were in fact ordinary lab rats. The results showed that the students unconsciously influenced the performance of the smart rats and from this drew the conclusion that similar things may be happening in classrooms. Similar experiments were held in a classroom scenario where, after random testing, teachers were told that certain students were expected to learn more quickly than others in the class and they were labelled 'academic bloomers'. A further test was issued at the end of the study to see if the academic bloomers had in fact progressed more than the other students; this hypothesis was proven by the test results, which showed a significant increase in the bloomers' test scores. The conclusions were used to illustrate the Pygmalion effect, which posits that performance is better when greater expectations are placed on individuals. This is usually explained by the different ways in which we might behave towards people for whom we have high expectations, for example there may be a higher level of interaction with them, they may be provided with extensive feedback to help develop their performance or they may simply be given more approval. The theory suggests that positive expectations of students influenced their performance in a positive way, whereas negative expectations influenced it negatively: 'When we expect certain behaviours of others, we are likely to act in ways that make the expected behaviour more likely to occur' (Rosenthal and Babad 1985:36).

In the mentoring context we need to be aware of the impact of our expectations on mentees because, consciously or not, we let them know what these expectations are. Within any given interaction we may exhibit lots of cues, such as a head tilt or the raising of eyebrows, all of which impact on the meaning of the communication to the other person. In this case, it makes some sense to think about how we might verbalise our expectations in ways that will have positive, rather than negative, outcomes.

Positive labelling

Praise and encouragement can be effective tools in building confidence but it is important to think about how we are using praise with mentees. The work of Carol Dweck (2008) on mindset also considered the impact of using praise in relation to abilities. In this study students were given easy IQ tests to complete and, when they had finished them, some of the students were praised for their ability, for example 'You did great, you must be really good at this', and others were praised for their effort 'That's a good score, you must have tried really hard'. The complexity of the tests was increased and this had an interesting impact on the students who had initially been praised for their ability. When faced with the more difficult tests, these students were less willing to take the risk of a bigger challenge, which might threaten their position of being talented, whereas the other group wanted the more challenging task so that they could learn from it. At the end of the study both groups of students were asked to write down their thoughts and their scores for the tests. A surprising finding was that almost 40% of the 'ability-praised' children lied about their scores: 'and always in one direction. In the fixed mindset, imperfections are shameful – especially if you're talented – so they lied them away' (Dweck 2008:73).

To avoid the negative impact of positive labelling, it is important that praise and encouragement are used in the right way. Some things to consider are:

- Address the action rather than the person, for example 'You did a great job', rather than 'You are great at this'.
- Recognise the effort that has gone into a particular action: 'You must have worked really hard on that.'
- Encourage inner direction, rather than the seeking of approval: 'What are you most proud of in this?' rather than 'I am proud of you for ….'

Congruence

As outlined in Chapter 2, congruence is an important factor in building rapport and as such is also fundamental when you are trying to establish a nurturing environment for mentoring. The term is closely connected to a Rogerian approach to working in one-to-one helping relationships, and could also be referred to as 'genuineness'. According to Rogers (1986), such work should take place in a warm, friendly environment in which both parties are accepting of the other. These seem like obvious factors within mentoring, but we might also want to consider how we demonstrate congruence.

As mentioned earlier in the chapter, it is important to recognise all forms of communication when trying to understand what mentees are telling us. The same is true for mentees; not only will they be listening to our words, they will also be interpreting other subtle signals like tone of voice or gestures.

In order to be congruent we need all of those signals to be in alignment. So, for example, if you meet someone new and they tell you they really like you, would you expect that statement to be delivered in a snappy tone with little eye contact? Or would you expect a warm tone, eye contact and perhaps a smile? It is possible to say one thing and mean another and as we communicate with others we automatically seek out signs of genuineness. When the ways that we communicate are not aligned, this is an example of incongruence, something that is usually associated with people we don't trust.

Congruence within the mentoring relationship is dependent on the development of open and honest communication. Factors that may help to support this are the boundaries you initially set with your mentee and the agreement that you will work together in a way that is authentic. Taking a democratic approach to mentoring ensures that the mentor is not set up as the font of knowledge but as a co-enquirer. By recognising that mentors as well as mentees are learning and developing through the process, we create an environment in which both can be honest and open about their own mistakes as well as their successes. This in turn helps develop a congruent approach to the role, if mentors are not judged for their lack of perfection, then they too can feel comfortable with, and even celebrate, their imperfect selves.

A sprinkling of magic

The creation of a nurturing environment is essential for positive mentoring. If our mentees know that the mentoring process is a safe place in which they can discuss their concerns without fear of judgement, they are more likely to develop the skills and capabilities they need for success. This is about creating the space in which they can grow to their full potential and, unlike the Bonsai tree, are not simply pruned and contained to emulate a small version of someone else.

This chapter has considered the importance of non-judgemental communication and congruence within mentoring. In the same way that this supports the growth of mentees, it also allows mentors to experience their own evolution. By working towards congruent practice, we are also acknowledging our own need to be authentic as illustrated in the famous quote attributed to both Carl Jung and Joseph Campbell: 'The privilege of a lifetime is to become who you truly are.'[1]

Figure 5.1 A sprinkling of magic: creating a nurturing environment

Note

1 see www.goodreads.com/quotes/75948-the-privilege-of-a-lifetime-is-to-bec ome-who-you.

Suggested further reading

Dweck, C. (2008) *Mindset: The New Psychology of Success.* London: Random House Publishing.

References

Dweck, C. (2008) *Mindset: The New Psychology of Success.* London: Random House Publishing.
Hatfield, E., Caccioppo, J. T. and Rapson, R. L. (1994) *Emotional Contagion.* New York. Cambridge University Press.

Maté, G. (2009) *In the Realm of Hungry Ghosts, Close Encounters with Addiction*. Toronto: Vintage Canada.

Rogers, C. (1986) Carl Rogers on the Development of the Person-centered Approach. *Person-Centered Review*, 1(3): 257–259.

Rosenthal, R. and Babad, E. Y. (1985) Pygmalion in the Gymnasium. *Educational Leadership*, 43(1): 36–39.

Rosenthal, R. and Jacobsen, L. (1968) *Pygmalion in the Classroom*. New York: Holt, Rinehart & Winston.

6 | Communication

Is it possible that, through their ability to communicate, trees can establish what other trees require and provide for these needs? According to scientists, the mycorrhizal network based on underground root systems helps trees to interact in ways that ensure their survival. They do this through a labyrinth of fungal connection by transferring oxygen and nitrogen back and forth as part of a symbiotic survival process.

In this chapter, we explore the nature of communication – its power, limitations and influence within mentoring – and consider strategies that can be used to enhance communication between mentors and mentees.

Models, metaphors and mammals

According to the anthropologist Gregory Bateson: 'The essence and *raison d'être* of communication is the creation of redundancy, meaning, pattern, predictability, information, and/or the reduction of the random by "restraint"' (Bateson 1972:130–131). Language, by its very nature, is an abstract thing, something we have created in order to communicate meaning so that we might connect with each other, but is it the only way in which we connect? Bateson argues that all mammals can communicate without language (in the sense that humans might understand language) and they do so through the organs that interpret the senses, suggesting that having a formal system of communication such as language might be removing potential meaning and information. Take, for example, a barking dog: if we were to decipher whether or not the dog's barking might be threatening to us, we would look at its stance, how its tail was wagging, whether the fur on its neck was raised – but most of all we would observe the organs through which the dog senses its environment, its eyes, ears, nose and mouth. Communication overall is a system through which we may 'see', 'hear' or 'feel' a message and the language provides only one side of that interaction.

At a very basic level, how we communicate can be outlined by using simple metaphors, which commonly describe the process as a transmission, an interaction or a transaction. Shannon and Weaver's model (1963) provides the first of these because it takes a linear approach based on the functioning of radio and telephone technologies. This includes three key elements: the *sender*, the *channel* and the *receiver*. The sender would be the person with a message to communicate, who would encode this message into appropriate language, select a suitable channel for transmission, such as a telephone conversation, and the message would be decoded by the receiver – simple! In theory this is a straightforward process; in reality, however, there are several things that can create differences between the message being sent and the message being received. At a practical level this could be down to technology, such as a poor signal on your mobile phone, but also includes other factors that interfere with transmission. Shannon and Weaver (1963) used the term 'noise' to describe such interference, and such noise could be the clarity of the message or the method of transmission. Noise might also include aspects of paralanguage such as intonation, speed of speech or gestures.

Dimbleby and Burton (1998) describe human communication as a relationship or interaction and recognise that any form of communication is also a form of sharing. Their description of the communication process acknowledges the use of overt and covert messages, in that some messages are quite obvious whereas others are hidden. I would extend this idea to include messages that are sometimes not even in the conscious awareness of the sender. How often do you find yourself saying something you hadn't intended to say? Or wonder why you chose to use specific words and on reflection realised that there was a covert message you were also trying to convey. At the time you said 'the thing' it might not have been obvious why, but, on later reflection, you discovered a genuine reason for introducing it into a conversation. At a very practical level, I find this happens often when I am doing semi-structured interviews for research. When typing up the transcripts I sometimes notice that people talk about what is on their minds and this may or may not answer the actual question they were asked. This is perhaps why many people find the interview process quite cathartic; they are being listened to by someone who is genuinely interested in their thoughts and, from a researcher's point of view, it is surprising how often these seemingly divergent comments reveal an aspect of the research that takes it in new and interesting directions.

Communication is also bound by conventions that are socially and culturally constructed, and influence the decisions we make about a particular message, or the person conveying it. Think about how often we might make judgements about people based not only on what they say, the specific words and phrases they use, but also on how they say it. Language alone is somewhat flawed as a method of communication because its interpretation is so often dependent on a range of other factors. Words alone can take on different meanings depending on how they are used, the context in which they are used and, not least, the ways in which they are interpreted by the receiver. This interpretation is also affected by context, semantics and emotion.

Consider the following statements:
   'I didn't picture you doing that – congratulations!'
   'I love how you are so chilled about all the clutter in here.'
   'I love your shoes, they look so comfortable.'
   'You are looking really healthy at the moment.'
   'Is that your partner? Wow they're absolutely gorgeous!'
   If these statements were put to you, what messages would you actually be receiving?

Most of the statements are simple and do not convey complex messages; all suggest a compliment and at a superficial level they are all positive. However, depending on your perception of the sender, how you feel about yourself and the context in which the message is delivered, you may interpret each of them as something other than praise. Let's consider them again:

'I didn't picture you doing that – congratulations!'
I'm amazed you could actually achieve that!
'I love how you are so chilled about all the clutter in here.'
This place is a mess!
'I love your shoes, they look so comfortable.'
Seriously, you wore those? You could have made an effort!
'You are looking really healthy at the moment.'
You don't usually look healthy.
'Is that your partner? Wow they're absolutely gorgeous!'
What do they see in you?

Communication is not simple, even when we choose relatively plain language. Take the phrase 'I love you', for example; within our culture this has a very distinct meaning. The words convey adoration, bonding, togetherness, intensity – and love, and it is possible to convey all of these emotions and feelings in the space of three words (Sprecher 1999). Yet, these simple words have an immense power to change a relationship and the response to them has a significant influence on the interactions that follow. If the words were changed slightly, by the addition of another word, their meaning would alter dramatically: 'I love you too' confirms the sentiments of the first message and produces a strong bond between the two people, suggesting that follow-on interactions will almost certainly be positive. 'I love you but …' also represents a change in one simple word yet embodies a condition, which depending on its nature will influence the effectiveness of follow-on communication. The words themselves are more or less the same but the meaning we give to them is almost certainly culturally and emotionally interpreted.

Analysing transactional communication

According to Berne (1964), communication forms part of a transaction between people, which may be analysed in order to judge what 'ego state' an individual is in at the time of communicating. An ego state might be defined as a set of thoughts and feelings that are linked to behaviours. When we communicate we do so from a particular ego state and it is suggested that this influences the way in which we communicate as well as the response we get from others. Transactional analysis is the study of these interactions and its aim is to encourage effective communication by acknowledging and responding appropriately to ego states. The ego state model has three key parts:

1. Parent: this conveys the impression of nurturing (or in some cases controlling); there is a strong focus on the observance of rules and also the concept of superiority. This ego state is said to represent the things we may have learnt from parental figures, so might include the conveyance of care or the reinforcement of rules. For example, 'You must get that report finished tonight' or 'You should take a break for a few minutes.'

2. Adult: this state is linked to rationality and logic. There is a focus on independence and a thoughtful approach to problem solving. 'What time can you get the report finished by?' or 'What are your views on your workload?'

3. Child: when in this state there tends to be a dependency on others and in some situations rebellion against those in charge. This is often considered the most emotional ego state, for example 'It's not fair; you still haven't finished your report; what am I going to do?'

A simple way to remember these states is that the parent state is often referred to as the *taught* state because it links to ingrained messages we have absorbed from the parental figures in our lives. The adult state might be considered to be the *thought* state because this reflects our ability to be objective and rationalise events. Finally, the child state is often seen as the most emotional of the ego states and is therefore referred to as the *felt* state, suggesting that the emotional response will take precedence over other possible responses.

Within the mentoring context, indeed within most interactions, it is highly likely that we will experience communication from each of these ego states, perhaps even within the same conversation. What is important is that we maintain effective communication by increasing the number of *complementary* transactions and decreasing the number of *crossed* transactions.

A complementary transaction is one that runs parallel. This means that the communication has a natural, fluid feel about it. We communicate something and get a response that is expected. For example, you may have made a mistake at work, which means that something you are working on will be late; you explain this to your boss and the response is an acknowledgement of what they have been told and recognition that you are aware of the issue. However, if your boss were to respond by getting very angry, admonishing you or even storming out of the room, you might be surprised by this response; in this case it is likely that the transaction is not complementary but considered to be crossed. This will have a subsequent impact on further communication.

Crossed transactions occur when the response received is not that which was invited by the communicator. So in the example above, the initial communication about the mistake was from the adult ego state and the expectation would be for the response also to be from the adult. However, in the second example, the communication involved emotional language, and childlike behaviour, indicating that the response was from a child ego state, thereby creating a crossed transaction. Very often what happens is that the communicator will switch states in order to bring the transaction back to a complementary one. So, this could go two ways:

I have let this project slip a little and won't be able to finish it until tomorrow.

(Sender – adult)

That's OK, it happens to us all, if you could let me have it by lunchtime that would be great.

(Respondent – adult)

I have let this project slip a little and won't be able to finish it until tomorrow.

(Sender – adult)

What? How can you do this to me? It's just not fair . . ..

(Respondent – child)

Not fair, let me tell you what's not fair ... I always have to do more than the others and I am never given any support . . ..

(Sender – child)

Alternatively this interaction could be adapted by choosing another complementary response, such as parent. This might be achieved by saying something like 'Sometimes things in life aren't fair but we must do our best to get things done'. This is less emotional than the initial response, and is in fact complementary, although it is probably not the most effective reply within a workplace scenario, and it would be more efficient to choose a response that could bring the communication back to an adult-to-adult transaction, for example 'I understand that this creates difficulties for you and I will finish the report as soon as possible'.

Understanding communication in the form of transactions may be useful as a strategy for helping us interact more effectively. For most of us, communication patterns are well rehearsed and we will respond in similar ways to situations that are triggers for us. Being aware of ego states allows us to think about the impact of what and how we communicate as well as the response we are likely to get. As mentors it is important to encourage complementary communication in order to get mentees to open up. To use this approach effectively does take practice and the following tips may be helpful:

- Start noticing the ego states present in conversations – this is the first stage in familiarising yourself with the theory.
- Reflect on your own communication style and things that may trigger responses from particular ego states – this will allow you to prepare for conversations which may be more difficult for you.

• Plan transactions according to what you have to say and the most appropriate ego state to say this from.

But what happens if, despite your best efforts, you still come across a situation full of crossed transactions? In this case you need to find strategies to try to maintain complementary communication by shifting ego states. So, if you need to calm something down, you might want to use an adult state, which could include presenting some facts or asking some questions. Alternatively you could appeal to the nurturing parent in the other person and ask for their advice, or share your worries. Communicating from your child ego state might also be helpful in showing the funny side of a situation or demonstrating enthusiasm.

Awareness of how we are communicating as much as what we communicate is essential if we want our interactions to be open and honest, and it is important that mentors recognise their ability to change the pattern of a given interaction, rather than relying on mentees to do so.

Seven layers of dialogue

Communication comes in all shapes and sizes and the messages we experience on a daily basis also assume different levels of importance and meaning for us. According to Lancer et al. (2016) verbal communication can be split into distinctly different types including debate, which has a focus on persuading others to your point of view, and discussion, whereby the aim might be to reach some sort of consensus and dialogue that is aimed at achieving new meaning. The third of these categories is particularly useful in the mentoring context and has been further subdivided into a model indicating seven layers of dialogue, which represent the depth and impact of particular dialogical approaches. An overview is provided in Figure 6.1.

This model begins with social dialogue, which may account for many of our daily interactions and has a focus on showing an interest in others and learning about them. Social dialogue is often seen as

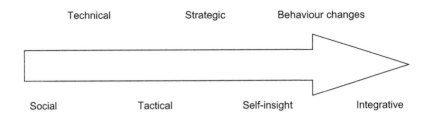

Figure 6.1 Seven layers of dialogue (adapted from Lancer et al. 2016)

essential to establishing rapport because it demonstrates recognition of others and provides a forum from which to share areas of common interest, thereby creating a connection. Social dialogue is important in the first stages of the mentoring relationship and helps to establish a way of working together. In this stage we might also employ technical dialogue in order to support the mentee's needs for essential information such as learning about processes and policies.

Tactical dialogue has a more pragmatic focus and its aim is to support the mentee in finding practical ways of dealing with particular issues or concerns. This is likely to be needed when your mentee comes to you with a specific problem in their work or personal life, such as juggling the responsibilities of home and work life, or coping with a difficult colleague. This type of communication would typically involve clarifying the situation, establishing ways forward, assessing potential barriers and developing an action plan, and might be something you would employ when setting goals and targets.

As well as the practical elements already highlighted, the model is also concerned with encouraging mentees to take a broader perspective in the form of strategic dialogue, whereby they might consider career development and the steps required to achieve their desired outcomes. This may involve considering a range of scenarios: what would happen if . . . or . . . what do you need to know or do to achieve . . .?, and could also employ practical tools such as a SWOT (strengths, weaknesses, opportunities, threats) analysis as a way of framing potential direction.

Perhaps the most powerful forms of dialogue outlined in this model are those that provide the opportunity for self-insight, which may in turn lead to behavioural change.

For the mentor these types of dialogue are about creating the space in which self-reflection can develop and mentees can use their insight, alongside learned strategies in order to adapt current thinking and behaviours. This might include creating a vision for potential outcomes as well as establishing how the mentee will know if they are making the desired progress. In very simple terms this could be summed up as 'What do you want to achieve?' and 'What will that look like?'. The final stage of integrative dialogue represents what might be viewed as the 'holy grail' of mentoring, indeed of any helping relationship. In this stage, the mentee gains a clear sense, not only of who they are but also of how they contribute to the overall organisation. This layer of dialogue could be seen as a vehicle for integrating different parts of the self, a sort of 'making whole' by bringing together cognitive, affective and behavioural aspects of the personality. It could be likened to notions identity, whereby the mentee has an insight into personal and professional roles and can make informed choices about what is right for them based on what they know about themselves. The mentor's role in this final layer of dialogue has been described as helping the mentee to write their story, including past, present and future aspects.

The importance of questions

The seven layers of dialogue presents a structure for mentor interventions in the helping role but some mentors may find it difficult to move to the final three layers of self-insight, behavioural change and integration, and it shouldn't be assumed that this is an easy, or even a natural, progression as the relationship develops. We all need a little help to guide our thinking and one useful strategy to support this process is the use of effective questioning.

Based on Socrates' ideas of teaching through questioning, the Socratic questioning method is an effective tool for influencing reflective thinking. This is based on six types of questions that help to clarify thinking, question assumptions and clear space for new insights. The first of these is conceptual clarification questions, based on a 'tell me more' approach, for example:

- Why are you saying that?
- What exactly does this mean?
- How does this relate to what we have been talking about?
- Can you give me an example?
- Are you saying ... or ...?

These questions prompt the respondent to think through their reasoning and make connections between concepts and real-life examples. It may also be useful to probe the assumptions that form the basis of unquestioned beliefs by using questions such as:

- How did you choose those assumptions?
- What else could we assume?
- How can you verify/disprove that assumption?

A third type of question used in the Socratic approach is one that probes rationale, reasons and evidence for particular arguments:

- How do you know this?
- Can you give me an example of that?
- What do you think causes ...?
- What evidence is there to support what you are saying? How might it be refuted?

Or, alternatively, you can use the approach to question viewpoints and perspectives:

- What alternative ways of looking at this are there?
- What is the difference between ... and ...?
- What would ... say about it?

This approach can be taken a step further by probing implications and consequences, which helps to check if understanding and assumptions make sense, for example:

* What are the implications of . . .?
* How does . . . affect . . .?
* How does . . . fit with what we learned before?

A final questioning strategy in the Socratic method is to ask questions about the question – in a sense this is simply turning the question in on itself, for example:

* What was the point of asking that question?
* Why do you think I asked you this question?

Using a Socratic approach allows us to challenge thoughts and assumptions in a constructive way; it also provides a foundation for deeper reflection on understandings as well as ingrained attitudes and behaviours. This may, in turn, provide the fuel for greater insight, which leads to behavioural change and integration.

Compassionate communication

An important aspect of mentoring is to ensure that the mentee feels supported within the relationship; effective communication is essential in this process. By exploring the transmission, interaction and transaction metaphors of communication we have considered the impact of relationship, context and paralanguage.

At the start of this chapter, language was referred to as a somewhat abstract vehicle for communicating messages, yet, within our culture, language assumes its own significance and for that reason it is also important to think about the actual words we choose. According to Newberg and Waldman (2013), in their aptly named book, *Words can change your brain*, words are not only a vehicle for translating messages, but also have the ability to form our reality in quite practical ways. Words, it is argued, can actually shape how we perceive reality: 'Human brains like to ruminate on negative fantasies, and they're also odd in another way: they respond to positive and negative fantasies as if they were real' (Newberg and Waldman 2013:27)

The research underpinning this book was used to identify strategies that would create compassionate communication, described by the authors as something that removes barriers such as defensiveness and increases harmonious interaction. This bond is referred to as 'neural resonance' and illustrates an enhanced form of communication in which both parties align themselves with each other. The twelve strategies for compassionate communication (Newberg and Waldman 2013:6) include:

1. Relax
2. Stay present
3. Cultivate inner silence
4. Increase positivity
5. Reflect on your deepest values
6. Access a pleasant memory
7. Observe non-verbal cues
8. Express appreciation
9. Speak
10. Speak slowly
11. Speak briefly
12. Listen deeply.

Many of these techniques relate to the skills we have discussed in previous chapters and some that are explored in more detail in later chapters. All have an impact on the effectiveness of our communication and although I wouldn't recommend using a 'template' approach to communicating with others, it is helpful to be mindful of the factors that will influence our interactions with others in positive ways.

A sprinkling of magic

A popular presupposition in neurolinguistic programming (NLP) is *the meaning of communication is the response you get*. This emphasises the importance of attending to our interactions with others, as well as becoming attuned to how mentees are interpreting the messages communicated to them. Communication is not only an interaction that impacts on our achievement, but also has a fundamental role to play in survival. We communicate with others to create bonds, establish communities and provide support, aspects of life that are fundamental to mentors and mentees alike.

Figure 6.2 A sprinkling of magic: communication

This chapter has considered the importance of effective communication in building mentoring relationships and the skills outlined will not only support mentoring practice but also have a significant impact on personal and professional relationships. Communicating effectively also provides mentors with opportunities to undertake their own behaviour change and integration by working towards congruent practice and the benefits of this cannot be underestimated.

Suggested further reading

Newberg, A. and Waldman, M. R. (2013) *Words Can Change Your Brain, 12 Conversation Strategies to Build Trust, Resolve Conflict, and Increase Intimacy.* New York: Plume.

Stewart, I. and Joines, V. (2003) *TA Today, A New Introduction to Transactional Analysis.* Kegworth: Lifespace Publishing.

References

Bateson, G. (1972) *Steps to an Ecology of Mind.* London: University of Chicago Press.

Berne, E. (1964). *Games People Play: The Basic Hand Book of Transactional Analysis.* New York: Ballantine Books.

Dimbleby, R. and Burton, G. (1998) *More than Words: An Introduction to Communication* (3rd edn). London: Routledge.

Lancer, N., Clutterbuck, D. and Megginson, D. (2016) *Techniques for Coaching and Mentoring* (2nd edn). Oxon: Routledge.

Newberg, A. and Waldman, M. R. (2013) *Words Can Change Your Brain, 12 Conversation Strategies to Build Trust, Resolve Conflict, and Increase Intimacy.* New York: Plume.

Schramm, W. (1954) *The Process and Effects of Communication.* Champaign, IL: University of Illinois Press.

Shannon, C. E. and Weaver, W. (1963) *The Mathematical Theory of Communication.* Champaign, IL: University of Illinois Press.

Sprecher, S. (1999) 'I Love You More Today than Yesterday': Romantic Partners' Perceptions of Changes in Love and Related Affect over Time. *Journal of Personality and Social Psychology,* 76(1): 46–53.

Modelling excellence

Trees are wonderfully symmetrical. They appear completely balanced, not only in terms of their own mass and growth direction but also in relation to each other. In forests they grow together and support each other and through their networks provide the nutrients and space each needs to survive. The mycorrhizal system, which has been referred to the 'wood-wide web' (BBC online) also provides a source of information and the ability for the tree community to develop social networks and learn from each other.

In this chapter, we explore social learning and the ways in which modelling others can be used as a technique to enhance development.

Social learning

Social learning theory is based on the premise that interaction with others plays a fundamental role in our development. According to Bandura (1977), as children we observe the people around us and through these observations learn particular behaviours. This is a form of social imitation that is not dissimilar to the way that other species learn; young animals, for example, quite naturally mimic the behaviours of the adults within their groups and through this process learn to fit in with the community. Similarly anyone who has observed young children will be very familiar with how apt they are at copying the behaviours they see, even the ones we may not want them to copy!

Bandura referred to this form of learning as modelling, a term that emphasises the importance of role models from whom we might learn. His famous Bobo doll experiments were set up to investigate how certain behaviours could be acquired through observation and imitation. In these experiments, children observed adult role models acting aggressively towards a Bobo doll and when left alone with the doll the children imitated this behaviour, suggesting to Bandura that: 'Most human behaviour is learned observationally through modelling: from observing others one forms an idea of how new behaviours are performed and on later occasions this coded information serves as a guide for action' Bandura (1977:22). Unlike behaviourist theory (based on the work of Pavlov, Watson, Skinner and others), modelling does not necessarily rely on the use of positive or negative reinforcement to initiate behaviours. Instead it is suggested that, in order to successfully reproduce behaviours an individual must be encouraged to pay attention to them, remember what they have seen and have the capacity and motivation to reproduce the behaviours in a similar context.

Mentors as role models

In terms of social learning, it is possible, if not probable that we will learn both positive and negative things and this is something that mentors need to be mindful of. Part of the job description for a mentor is to act as a role model for mentees. Indeed, within most mentoring programmes, it is people who demonstrate the desired skills in a particular occupation who are selected as mentors, suggesting that the framework of mentoring is based on modes of social and situated learning. However, we also need to acknowledge that mentors cannot be experts in everything, and it might even be argued that general 'experts' probably don't make the best mentors, because a significant part of mentoring is the ability to empathise with others, something that might be difficult for those rare individuals who are good at everything! This means that, at some point, if not at several points in their mentoring career, most mentors will be expected to guide mentees to develop skills or abilities that they don't themselves possess and must look to others to help reinforce this development. The mentor's role here is to act as a conduit between the two parties, something that represents the networking element of the role outlined in the models of mentoring described in Chapter 1.

Modelling excellent practice

A basic premise of neurolinguistic programming (NLP) is that everything has a structure, thereby creating form that may be studied and imitated or adapted. The NLP concept of modelling is founded on this principle and suggests that it is possible to reproduce 'excellence' through a deliberate process of imitation. Simply put, this means developing the specific skills demonstrated by others through adopting the strategies they do in a very structured and purposeful way.

A starting point for this technique is to make explicit the differences between someone who is excellent at a particular skill and someone who is not. This is followed by a detailed study of the patterns and processes associated with the particular skill in order to replicate the language, thoughts and behaviours related to it. At a superficial level this seems like a simple enough process, but what happens when someone is so skilled at something that they don't actually know how they do what they do?

Think about skills you have, simple everyday things that you might do automatically. Are any of those skills things that friends or acquaintances might find difficult to do? A simple example might be something like making an omelette: this is a relatively straightforward task, and you can follow a recipe to help you, but it is also something that seems to cause concern to people who don't view themselves as cooks. Can you list the various steps you take to carry out the particular task that you can do with ease?

How easy was that activity for you? For some practical skills it is perhaps easier to describe an action or outline a sequence of events, and you may do this by recalling some of your initial learning, or you may remember being given lessons or someone demonstrating the skill to you and can use this as a template to teach others. This process will, however, be far less simple for things that fall in to the category of 'soft skills'. If, for example, you are particularly accomplished at creating rapport with strangers, or getting people to open up to you, or coming up with creative ideas, how do you do that? Are you consciously aware of taking specific steps to achieve these aims? Have you even bothered to think about it, or do you just gratefully accept that this is something you can do? For less practical skills such as these there may well be a number of nuanced behaviours that you have developed over the years without even being aware of it, and this will make it far more difficult for you to explain your strategies to others.

It is possible that, for some everyday tasks, you have developed a level of unconscious competence that allows you to carry out particular activities without even being aware of how you do so. A model developed by Burch (cited in Bates 2016) describes this process as the conscious–unconscious model, which represents four stages of learning a skill:

1. Stage 1 – unconscious incompetence: a stage that includes doing things wrong but not being aware that they are wrong.

2. Stage 2 – conscious incompetence: still getting some things wrong but aware that this is the case.

3. Stage 3 – conscious competence: doing things right but having to think about them consciously.

4. Stage 4 – unconscious competence: doing things right and not having to think about it.

There are many everyday abilities that fall into this category such as riding a bike or driving a car, yet, just like any of these activities, there is a structure in place. Take the example of cooking an omelette: you have to break eggs, chop ingredients, warm the pan and so on. It is also necessary to follow these steps in a particular order if you want to achieve success. So, if people are demonstrating skills and abilities that they carry out with a degree of unconscious competence, they are unlikely to be able to explain or make obvious what it is they are doing. If this is the case, how are others able to model that particular skill or behaviour? A simple answer to this would be to use a structured approach to modelling which is outlined in the following 10-step plan:

1. Select a desired skill or behaviour and one or more 'models' who exhibit these skills, make contact with the relevant person/people and arrange to observe them 'in action'.

2. During the observation try to locate a sequence of events, for example, first they do this, then they do that ... followed by this, followed by ... and so on until you feel confident you have noted every step.

3. Write down any questions to ask the model about what you have observed, for example how do you know when to do this? What happens first? What happens next? How do you know that you have finished? Why do you do ...? Or ...? Is there a reason for ...? There may be things the model isn't even aware of, so it is really important to list all of your questions.

4. After you have observed and then met with your model to reflect on your questions, rewrite the sequence of events you outlined in step 2.

5. Arrange another observation of the model so that you can check and amend the sequence of events.

6. Picture yourself carrying out the sequence. Try to disassociate yourself and simply observe what you do as if you were looking from the outside in.

7. Imagine yourself following the sequence, this time fully associated. What do you think as you work though? How do you feel? What specifically do you notice?

8. Carry out the sequence for real. Don't think about it too much, just do it. Repeat the process as many times as you can.

9. Ask your model to observe you carrying out the sequence and provide feedback on what you do.
10. Use the feedback to refine the sequence.

It is important to have an awareness of the conscious steps taken to complete a given activity, but it is likely that those things the 'modeller' is doing with unconscious competence are very important to success and therefore need to be observed and noted carefully; so, if you are not confident that you have captured those steps, it is important to go through the process again so that you can locate them. This isn't a magical formula, of course; it is simply a model you can use to structure the process of imitating excellent behaviours. It is likely that you will not discover all the things you need to know by simply going through these steps once; as with many things, the process of learning new things takes time and patience, as outlined in the wisdom of *Alice in Wonderland*: 'Begin at the beginning', the king said gravely, 'and go till you come to the end; then stop' (Carroll 1998:ix).

The NLP modelling technique is about finding a structure to a particular activity, so you may well be imitating actions but you will also be selecting the essential features of the activity and representing them in ways that work for you. Modelling is not a miracle solution to a problem; it is a simply a strategy that may help to build a repertoire of tools you can use and this itself is very helpful.

Pro-social modelling

In Chapter 5 we discussed the concept of pro-social behaviours and described these as behaviours that were focussed on helping other people such as sharing, cooperating or supporting. Originally proposed as an antidote to antisocial behaviour, pro-social behaviours have a focus on demonstrating positive behaviours to others and as such form one of the foundations of the mentoring role. Although mentors may be appointed on the basis of their experience and expertise, one aspect of the role is helping mentees to adapt to their environment by modelling the behaviours that will help them to do so. These might include respect for others' opinions, collaborating with colleagues, being punctual, and so on, but it is possible that there are also some specific behaviours that will be helpful in your own context and it is important that these are demonstrated to mentees to give them every chance of success. According to Hall et al. (2008) mentors are expected to give positive feedback and encouragement, share ideas, suggestions and strategies, guide and direct, and model good practice. Mentors are also expected to challenge their mentees and create awareness of specific areas for development and this may involve relating sensitively to mentees in ways that build trust and confidence in order to enable them to reflect honestly on their practice. Mentors are indeed role models but it is also important to remember that they should not be seen as the only model of professional practice; indeed one important aspect of mentoring is emphasising collaboration and learning from each other. The purpose of mentoring is not the creation of the 'mini-me' practitioner but the vehicle through which mentees may discover their own effective practice.

Graeme is a new recruit to the organisation and you have recently been appointed as his mentor. One thing you are becoming increasingly aware of is how dismissive Graeme is of his colleagues; he often makes derisory comments about their work and openly shares his comments about how out of date he feels many work practices are. Even in the short time you have been working with Graeme, you have noticed that he is struggling to build rapport with the people with whom he works closely, and you are very conscious that his role involves working in collaboration with many of his colleagues, so the ability to create rapport and a strong sense of teamwork is essential to his success. It is time to address this concern and you need a strategy that will help Graeme to develop the skills he needs.

How would you model the behaviours you would like Graeme to develop? What strategies might you employ to demonstrate the effectiveness of building strong collaborative relationships with colleagues? There are a number of approaches you could take, such as encouraging observation of peers, getting Graeme involved in working with cohesive teams, opening up a dialogue about what he notices about how others work together and so on. By introducing ideas about collaboration and collegiality, it will be possible to highlight specific areas for development, which in turn may create an opening for Graeme to select his own models of good practice and use the modelling technique to develop skills in working with others. This part of the process is key as Graeme must be the one to notice, and act on, perceived areas for development; he may not see things the way that you see them but could be encouraged to analyse his own perceptions by observing others and expanding his ideas about what 'good practice' entails.

The difference that makes the difference

It is very tempting when using approaches such as modelling, to work on the assumption that there is a specific 'thing' that makes all the difference to the results we get. This thing might be words, attitudes, actions or even beliefs and, in the example of modelling provided in this chapter, something that takes place at a level of unconscious competence. Seeking that specific 'difference' is not something new; in fact it probably fuels a great number of self-help books which in turn may well make a difference to their readers – or not.

Gregory Bateson is often accredited with the quote 'Information is a difference that makes a difference' (Azquotes) which is a powerful indicator that we need to seek information in order to change the impact of our actions, and the modelling technique certainly goes some way to providing that information. The quote is based on the idea that we are all part of a system that is closely linked by a range of cause-and-effect relationships, suggesting that a change in one thing will have a ripple effect on other changes. For example, a nasty rumour about a person may spread throughout a community and cause that person to be shunned, or even attacked. In this example, the rumour might be classed as the thing that made the difference because, without it, it is unlikely that the shunning/attacking events would have taken place. These ideas are based on cybernetics' systems theory, which aims to understand the purposes and processes of systems and the causal chains that work within them. Another of Bateson's famous quotes makes clear his belief that we are all part of such systems: 'What is the pattern that connects the crab to the lobster and the primrose to the orchid, and all of them to me, and me to you?' (Bateson 1979:8); this belief may be a sound basis for the use of modelling in order to achieve excellence. In a sense, by following a structure to model excellence, what we are looking for is the pattern that connects.

These are powerful and, it has to be said, very attractive ideas – and they certainly have their place in the mentoring relationship but it is important that, as with many techniques and models, the strategies are explored within a relevant context. Bateson's quote about information is actually misquoted; in his book *Steps to an Ecology of Mind* the quote is: 'A "bit" of information is definable as a difference which makes a difference' (Bateson 1972:315). This suggests that we might not be seeking a single thing in order to enact change, but that a single thing could make a difference within a given context, and in turn that context and the people within it will influence the impact of the action. Bateson is clear on the impact of environment as well as perception: 'Cybernetically speaking "my" relation to any larger system around me and including other things and persons will be different from "your" relation to some similar system around you' (Bateson 1972:332). This suggests that context and individual perceptions of it have a significant influence on the way we experience events.

So what does this mean for the mentor and the mentee, and even the mentoring relationship overall? A central consideration is the importance of collaborative inquiry, in that evaluation and discovery of new approaches will be a shared process. It also suggests that we cannot seek immediate change by implementing a single technique; rather we should generate an awareness of the impact of environmental factors on the strategies we choose to adopt, as well taking into account practical considerations that relate to our specific context.

The modelling strategy is a useful technique for developing new skills but is more effective overall if combined with sensible reflective practice, because the purpose is to find approaches that work for you, rather than simply adopting others' practice. Through reflection on and evaluation of our own practice we create a foundation for discussion and opportunities for exploration of a wide range of strategies. This in turn generates possibilities for change, but only if we are genuinely open to those possibilities.

Values, thoughts and mindset

Our individual approaches to developing professional skills may be influenced by a number of things such as self-efficacy, core values and general beliefs, which in turn will provide stimuli for specific behaviours and determine how we apply ourselves to personal and professional challenges. There is a well-known quote by Gandhi which expresses this idea fluently:

> *Your values become your thoughts*
> *Your thoughts become your words,*
> *Your words become your actions,*
> *Your actions become your habits,*
> *Your habits become your values,*
> *Your values become your destiny.*
> (cited in Thompson and
> Wolstencroft 2018)

Our values and beliefs certainly have an impact on how we approach change or specific challenges, particularly those beliefs related to our own self-efficacy. As outlined in Chapter 5, mindset is a term used to describe individual beliefs about achievement and is based on the work of Carol Dweck (2008) as a result of her research into achievement and success. Dweck suggests that success has more to do with our approach to something than our innate talents or abilities and proposes that there are key differences in attitudes towards challenge. The main differences are based on an individual's belief about their ability to succeed and Dweck outlines two groups: those with a 'fixed mindset' based on the belief that intelligence, qualities and talents are fixed and cannot be changed, and those with a 'growth mindset' in which there is a belief that abilities can be developed through dedication and hard work. This work has had a huge influence on classrooms around the world because it provides a powerful insight into the importance of attitude and motivation in relation to achievement. In simple terms, if we can change our attitude, then we can change our ability to achieve. Based on this premise it is easy to see why the concept is so popular with educators.

It is possible to consider mindset as some sort of panacea in that all we have to do is believe we can do things, apply ourselves to the tasks at hand and, as if by magic, we will be successful; it is worth remembering, however, that developing a growth mindset isn't just about our efforts, which is a common misconception. Just applying more effort to something will not necessarily mean you will be successful, particularly if the effort is misdirected. If you are learning to play a musical instrument, you may choose to put in hours of practice, but if your hours of practice do not involve performing the techniques that will produce the desired sound, is your practice useful, or does it have the potential to reinforce strategies that are not helping you to progress? The desire to achieve something, followed by a certain amount of effort, are certainly sensible aspirations, but we also need to try out new strategies and seek guidance when we are stuck on something. We need to remember that effort is a means to an end on which it should be focused in order to achieve a specific learning goal, so simply trying our best isn't enough and, if what we are doing isn't working, we need to try something else. The notion of a growth mindset was developed to help close achievement gaps and therefore must include acknowledging the truth about current achievements as well as considering different strategies to reach intended goals. This is so much more than simply applying a bit more effort.

Encouraging your mentee to develop the attitude of applied effort is certainly a good thing, especially when it is closely related to honest evaluation and seeking new approaches. This, coupled with strategies for modelling excellent practice, will provide the impetus for effective change. However, the important thing to remember is that it is not about categorising behaviours as 'growth' or 'fixed' mindset approaches, but about accepting the current situation (which includes acceptance that we probably all have fixed and growth mindsets in different contexts) and being open to trying new behaviours which may bring about change. Although the theory is sometimes seen as something of a quick fix – have the right mental attitude and all will be well – Dweck emphasises that it is actually about seeking challenge, being intrigued by mistakes and enjoying the process of finding a better way. If we were to seek the difference that might make a difference, perhaps attitude towards challenge and change might be a positive starting point.

A sprinkling of magic

Guiding mentees through the process of change can be one of the most challenging and rewarding things a mentor does and is a

Figure 7.1 A sprinkling of magic: symbiotic development

significant part of the role. In the same way that trees support each other through the mycorrhizal network, mentors support their charges by creating connections to others and easing the course of developmental change. In doing so, mentors also open themselves up to opportunities for new learning. Simply by developing an awareness of where they can and cannot model excellence for their mentee, the mentor is provided with the opportunity to seek out new ways of doing things for themselves and in this way change within the mentoring relationship is a form of symbiotic development.

In this chapter we have explored approaches to modelling the excellence displayed by others and considered the ways in which habits of thinking can impact on how we tackle challenges and change. Whatever strategies are adopted, achieving excellence appears to have its foundations in both attitude and effort and may be linked to the development of excellent habits: 'Excellence is an art won by training and habituation: we do not act rightly because we have virtue or excellence, but we rather have these because we have acted rightly; . . . we are what we repeatedly do' (Durrant 1926:76). This notion, coupled with a recognition of the need to direct effort appropriately, creates the foundation for achieving excellence in our practice; if we are what we repeatedly do, then we need to do the things that help us to achieve our aspirations.

Suggested further reading

Bandler, R., Roberti, A. and Fitzpatrick, O. (2013) *The Ultimate Introduction to NLP, How to Build a Successful Life*. London: Harper Collins.
Bateson, G. (1972) *Steps to an Ecology of Mind*. London: University of Chicago Press.

References

Azquotes. Available at: www.azquotes.com/author/1040-Gregory_Bateson [date accessed 4 March 2018].
Bandura, A. (1977) *Social Learning Theory*. Englewood Cliffs, NJ: Prentice
Bates, B. (2016) *Learning Theories Simplified*. London: Sage.
Bateson, G. (1972) *Steps to an Ecology of Mind*. London: University of Chicago Press.

Bateson, G. (1979) *Mind and Nature, a Necessary Unity*. New York: E. P. Dutton.

BBC online. Available at: www.bbc.com/earth/story/20170109-plants-can-see-hear-and-smell-and-respond [date accessed 6 March 2018].

Carroll, L. (1998) *Alice's Adventures in Wonderland and through the Looking-Glass and What Alice Found There* (The Centenary Edition). London: Penguin Classics.

Durrant, W. (1926) *The Story of Philosophy*. New York: Simon & Schuster Inc..

Dweck, C. S. (2008) *Mindset the New Psychology of Success*. New York: Ballantine

Hall, K. M., Draper, R. J., Smith, L. K. and Bullough, R. V. (2008) More than a Place to Teach: Exploring the Perceptions of the Roles and Responsibilities of Mentor Teachers. *Mentoring and Tutoring: Partnership in Learning*, 16 (3): 328–345

Thompson, C. and Wolstencroft, P. (2018) *The Trainee Teachers Handbook, a Companion for Initial Teacher Training*. London: Learning Matters.

8 | Challenging

The evidence relating to plant communication may be relatively new but people have talked to plants for many years and a recent study by the Royal Horticultural Society suggests that this practice actually helps plants to grow. Trees take this one step further by 'talking' to each other, using signalling to indicate threats and to acknowledge siblings (Gorzelak et al. 2015). If such communication is to be effective then it must encompass aspects of challenge as well as reinforcement. When you talk to plants, should you simply tell them how well they are doing, or maybe challenge them to do better?

In this chapter, we explore the ways in which mentors use challenge to help mentees achieve their aims. We discuss the importance of feedback and strategies you can use to challenge types of 'unhelpful' thinking, as well as establishing the right amount of challenge for the individual.

The importance of feedback

In the context of education, Black and Wiliam (1998) make reference to the use of formative assessment to provide feedback to students and refer to this as evidence that can be used to enhance performance. In their study they found what they referred to as a 'poverty of practice' whereby the focus was on giving marks or making comparisons, rather than on providing guidance on development. By taking this approach teachers were focusing on assessment of current achievement, rather than potential improvements, and in doing so were inadvertently limiting the potential of students. Feedback in mentoring is important for a number of reasons:

- It provides an opportunity to highlight what mentees do well;
- It helps to build rapport between mentor and mentee;
- It can help to build the mentee's confidence in relation to their performance or development.

But, perhaps most importantly, feedback provides the opportunity to explore development potential and instigate positive change. For this reason, feedback must also include challenge. It is readily acknowledged that positive mentoring is based on the foundations of rapport and trust, and many mentors see a main function of their role as being the channel through which change can occur. This indirect influence can sometimes make it difficult for mentors to challenge their mentees because they may be focused on maintaining the rapport and trust they have already built, and throwing challenge into that mix will inevitably disturb the equilibrium. In Chapter 2 we discussed the levels of rapport consistent with the mentoring relationship and, although some mentors may veer towards the 'warmer' end of this scale, the aim is to maintain overall positive regard for your mentee, a requirement of which is to challenge where appropriate. Without this, there is a danger that you become complicit in maintaining current practice and do not offer your mentee the opportunity to develop to their full potential.

Providing constructive feedback

Constructive feedback represents information that supports personal and professional growth so it is fundamental within mentoring. There are a number of approaches that can be taken to structure feedback but a key point to remember is that the focus is on development rather than measurement, as outlined in Table 8.1.

Table 8.1 Judgemental versus constructive feedback

Judgemental feedback	Constructive feedback
Makes comparisons with others and may include a form of grading	Is based on clear criteria and provides information about the extent to which these have or have not been met
Can make less confident mentees nervous and less likely to take risks for fear of 'failure'	Increases feelings of acceptance and acknowledgement that efforts are being recognised
Level of emotional involvement in task increases
May increase 'maladaptive' and surface learning approaches because the focus is on the grade/need to pass rather than fail
Generates a 'right answer' syndrome	Focus on gaining information about improvements increases effective learning approaches
An increase in self-esteem comes from effort and the promotion of independence
Generates a sense of blaming – mistakes become shameful	Generates a blame-free culture – mistakes become opportunities to learn
Can reduce interest, effort and persistence as well as self-belief	Can increase interest, effort, persistence as well as self-belief
May increase 'learned helplessness' and hostility towards learning
Or, in the case of those mentees who achieve good grades, may increase complacency	Increases resourcefulness in seeking the right approaches and accepting that effort in learning has a positive impact
Learning is seen as something for others – it is all about the judgement	Learning is seen as an end in itself – the judgement is far less important.

Using the feedback sandwich

Although I would always recommend taking into account context, communication styles and individual preferences when communicating with your mentee, it can sometimes be helpful to structure the communication in ways that are likely to achieve the desired outcome. As discussed earlier in the chapter, communication with, and feedback to, your mentee are best structured using a non-judgemental and formative approach. We will discuss two particular techniques that will be helpful in providing this structure: the 'feedback sandwich' and the 'skilled helper' model.

The feedback sandwich works on the basis of praising what has been done well, followed by information about what could have been better. In effect it is about 'sandwiching' criticism between two positive points, for example:

> You did a great job in organising the last customer event. The budget was over by 30%, so we need to look at more effective ways of keeping this on track. I understand you worked hard on ensuring everything ran smoothly and you did a great job on that.

> You handled that group really well and the lesson went according to plan. Did you notice the girl on the right-hand side? She seemed to be struggling with the activities and I wondered if you could find a way of supporting her more. Excellent planning overall.

This strategy provides a structure for giving an overall impression of your feedback as well as an opportunity to clarify misunderstandings, or things that could be improved, finally finishing on a note of praise which is intended to improve motivation and reception to feedback.

> Consider the examples provided above and try to think of occasions when you might have been influenced by the feedback sandwich technique as a recipient, or indeed when you have used this method for structuring feedback. What were the benefits of this approach? What might be the drawbacks?

Using a 'formulaic' approach to structuring feedback certainly has its benefits but it is not something that must be followed slavishly, and it is important to remember that feedback should be part of overall development. This means that we need to be very clear in the information we are providing and ensure that the points linked to development are not hidden within the overall praise. A key component of feedback is that it is honest and specific and, for these reasons, models used to structure feedback must be adapted to suit individual contexts. The praise sandwich method has been subject to some criticism because it may undermine the value of information that is important to an individual's development. If development points are 'sandwiched' between two comments including praise, it is possible that some people will not always hear what it is they need to do in order to improve. If you were to take the approach literally and be completely honest with your mentee, you may in fact be saying something along the lines of:

> I have some negative feedback for you but I am going to start with some positive points to make you feel better, then I will discuss the points I really want to get to and I'll end on something positive so that you won't be upset or angry with me.

Clearly this approach would not be helpful, so it is important to remember that this is a strategy that should be used with care.

The skilled helper

Another approach to structuring feedback is the 'skilled helper model' (Egan 1998). This is a three-stage model that was originally developed to help people solve problems, as well as consider potential opportunities. It could be defined as a way of helping people to help themselves, because it is based on empowering the individual to find their own solutions.

The skilled helper model aims to address three key questions:

1. What is going on?
2. What do I want instead?
3. How might I get what I want?

So this model considers the current situation, the preferred situation and potential strategies to help move from one to the other. In this way it is a very practical and focused approach, which can be combined with setting specific goals.

What is going on?

In the first stage of the model, the aim is to discover what is going on for your mentee. This will involve providing a safe space for your mentee to explain their story in their own way. What is really important at this point is making sure that the other person feels heard, so you must avoid the temptation to jump in with solutions or stories of your own. Some specific strategies that may be helpful are active listening, checking understanding, reflecting, summarising and using open questions, and you may find it useful to review some of the skills outlined in previous chapters.

Sometimes it can be difficult for a mentee to see their situation clearly, or from different angles, because they are emotionally involved in it. If your mentee experiences these types of 'blind spots' it is important to encourage reflection through the use of open questions. This will provide the space for a more objective assessment of a given situation and will also help to avoid a sense of being stuck. To move things forward you could try questions such as 'What in all of this is the most important to you?' or 'What would make the most difference?'.

What do I want instead?

When you both have a clear sense of the 'story', the next stage is to assess what your mentee would like to change. In this phase of the model the aim is to move from problem to potential action, and it is important to help establish what your mentee really wants to change before looking at any specific strategies to implement change. A skill that would be useful at this stage is the facilitation of imaginative thinking through activities such as brainstorming or mind-mapping. This provides the scope to explore a range of ideas before deciding on the desired outcome.

How might I get what I want?

The final stage of the model represents the practical, goal-setting part of the process. Once the desired outcome has been established and goals have been outlined, it is worth testing whether the goals are ecological, in that they fit with the mentee's overall aim or vision for development. Goals that do not lead to ecological outcomes are unlikely to be achieved or maintained, so this is an important aspect of overall goal setting. One way of checking whether or not an outcome is ecological is by exploring the costs and the benefits, which you could do by asking the following questions:

- What will be the benefits when you achieve this?
- How will it be different for you when you've done this?
- What will be the costs of doing this?
- Any disadvantages/downsides to doing this?

It is also important to consider specific strategies for achieving goals by using questions such as:

- How many different ways are there for you to do this?
- Who/what might help?
- What has worked before/for others?
- What about some wild ideas?

This may well generate more strategies than are needed, so it is useful to take a pragmatic approach and try to find the best fit. Some useful questions might be: 'Which of these ideas appeals most?' or 'Which are within your control?' At this point both parties will be ready to move the planning to action, so encourage this by asking: 'What will you do first?', 'When and what will you do next?'

It might be useful to give some thought to the most appropriate format for using the skilled helper model. If you want to record goals, do you want to use some form of goal-setting template or an action plan, or would a mind-map be appropriate? It would also be useful to discuss how you are going to review progress in relation to the goals so that you can measure the success of planned actions.

Logical levels of feedback

One suggested 'rule' of feedback is to ensure that you are commenting on specific behaviour not on traits. So you might be providing feedback on how your mentee handled a particular situation or interaction. If you were to follow this rule, the feedback would be objective and state what was observed; this may mean it included a number of 'I' statements to demonstrate that objectivity, for example 'I noticed that when you did this ... the response was ... that'. Taking this approach ensures that you are not making any judgements in relation to capability, attitude or values. However, as the mentoring relationship progresses it may well become more difficult to separate the person from the behaviour, and it may even be beneficial to open up discussion about how behaviours might be influenced by things that are more personal, such as beliefs, attitudes and emotions.

The notion of 'logical levels' (Dilts 2014 – see www.nlpu.com/Articles/LevelsSummary.htm) is based on the idea that many processes are created by the relationships between systems, in that one action causes another reaction, suggesting that nothing occurs in complete isolation. In a practical sense this means that when we behave in certain ways, those behaviours influence and are influenced by other things. This could be represented as a hierarchy of levels, each of which has the role of synthesising, organising or directing the level below it. So, in the context of behaviour change, if we were to change something at an upper level, that change would impact on lower levels within the hierarchy. For example, a perception that we don't possess certain skills and deem ourselves incapable, or of limited capability, in a particular area may generate a belief that we can't do something. A common example of this is people who say they can't draw or can't do maths. This in turn becomes part of our sense of self and in order to maintain this we are likely to avoid situations that call upon our 'limited skills'. For this reason, if we want changes to be effective, it is useful to understand which logical levels mentees may be focusing on when they are discussing or planning change. The levels outlined by Dilts include:

1. Environment
2. Behaviour
3. Capabilities
4. Beliefs and values
5. Identity.

Spirituality may also be included in the logical levels but is considered to be a step beyond the individual, in that it represents the relationship to a bigger system. If spirituality were to be included in your model of logical levels then this would appear as the first item, above identity.

The use of logical levels within coaching and mentoring is helpful in trying to fully understand the current situation, which in turn will lead to finding the most appropriate strategies for change.

Environment refers to the external conditions in which we operate. If a mentee is operating at this level they are likely to provide explanations on what happened, who was there and other contextual details. It is unlikely that the story will be about them; it is more likely to be focused on the event.

Behaviour is the actions or reactions of a particular individual within the environment, so your mentee may describe what they did or thought and the impact of these.

Capability or competence might be thought of as the 'how-to' level. If your mentee describes their story by talking about how they could achieve something, or what specific skills they might need to do so, they are focused on their capability/competence.

Belief relates to why something happened or was done in a particular way. This might also be linked to values. If the story is focused on reasons behind behaviours, including any specific beliefs or values, this is an indicator.

Identity links to a sense of self and to aspects of self-actualisation or what makes the person tick.

> Gretchen is talking about the behaviour of one of her direct reports. She is describing a number of incidents in which the person demonstrated childish behaviour towards other team members, which she felt was creating a barrier with the rest of the team and making it difficult for them to work well together. Gretchen feels she must find a solution to the problem and is discussing ways in which she has tried to encourage different behaviour, but she is not sure what impact this has had and feels she is getting stuck. Gretchen has expressed concern about her ability to generate the necessary change within the team and feels this is because she is not assertive enough as a manager.

Can you identify which of the logical levels Gretchen is occupying? Is it the environment? Gretchen is reporting a story about someone else's behaviour so it certainly has elements of this level, and she also discusses her own behaviour within the environment by reflecting on the impact of her strategies. The final comment suggests that an unhelpful belief about her own capabilities – 'not assertive enough as a manager' – is what may be creating a sense of being stuck in the current situation. In Gretchen's view, she has already tried some strategies and her perceived lack of assertiveness may be what is holding her back from pursuing other avenues. If this is the case it is important for the mentor to challenge these assumptions by getting Gretchen to reflect on the impact of her perceptions. One way of doing this might be to use questions based on each of the levels to uncover the underlying beliefs in relation to Gretchen's perception of her own assertiveness. For example:

'If I was an observer what would I notice?' – this encourages reflection on specific factors in the environment.

'Think about your behaviour, what do you typically do in this situation?' (behaviour)

'Which of your skills are you using in this situation?' – are there any other skills you could use? (capability)

'What do you believe is happening in this situation?' – What do you believe about yourself and others? (beliefs)
'What is important to you in this situation?' (identity)

The use of these questions will elicit an alternative account of Gretchen's particular situation; they also move the discussion on to another level and provide a different perspective from which to view the incident. By uncovering what is important to Gretchen's identity, it may be possible to uncover some of the beliefs that may be causing her to be stuck. Even if that isn't the case, generating discussion at different levels will certainly lead to potential ideas for new strategies, and that in itself is a very useful outcome.

Using development goals

Within professional roles, most mentoring relationships are based on the premise that the process will encourage developmental change; as a result working with mentees to set developmental targets is often something that is built into the mentor's role. According to Locke and Latham (1990) the setting of clear goals has a significant impact on motivation and performance as long as the goals are specific and challenging. Most people are familiar with the SMART model for goal setting, but, just in case, this relates to Specific, Measurable, Achievable, Realistic and Timebound goals. As a guide to setting goals this provides a general framework, which can be useful, but how often have you seen it used in a really effective way? One of the issues with this framework might be the interpretation of the word 'realistic'; in my experience this is so often interpreted as 'easy' and as a result leads to the setting of goals that have so little challenge that they are not motivating for the individual.

Goals need to be challenging if they are to be motivating, if they aren't they have simply become tasks. According to Locke and Latham (1990) the need for challenging but not overwhelming goals is a key factor to success; they recommend five principles for effective goal setting:

- Clarity
- Challenge
- Commitment
- Feedback
- Task complexity.

To distinguish between something that is a goal rather than a task, it needs to be recognisable as important to overall development, not simply a part of day-to-day activities, so it should include a beginning, middle and end that outline the action, specific detail relating to that action and the outcome:

- Action: start with an active verb such as implement, design, produce.
- Specific detail: this is the 'what' and states exactly what should be achieved – 'design a process for recording professional development activities'.
- The outcome relates to something which is measurable: 'share details of process at team meeting on ….'

Deciding on what represents a challenge for someone is an important step in this process. We all respond to pressure differently; for some it is the motivation needed to progress, whereas others may become overwhelmed and as a result performance will suffer. The inverted U model, based on the work of Yerkes and Dodson (1908) (Figure 8.1), outlines this by showing the links between cognitive arousal and performance, suggesting that performance may increase as a result of pressure but only up to a point; when the pressure becomes too much for the individual, this leads to anxiety and poor performance.

What constitutes 'pressure' for individuals is likely to be affected by a number of influences such as:

- Skill level: does the individual have the relevant skills to complete the goal?

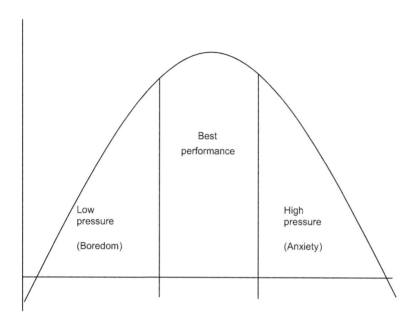

Figure 8.1 Inverted U model

- Personality: how do they normally respond to pressure? Are there signs of anxiety in relation to this?
- Complexity: how complex is the task?

In general, people can complete simple tasks while experiencing a reasonable amount of pressure, whereas complex tasks require low-pressure environments to provide the space for clear thinking.

You have two mentees who both have the same development need. Neither of them makes an effective contribution in team meetings. For one of your mentees this is a result of limited attention; she simply finds it difficult to focus on the meeting because she is often processing other ideas, and as a result she becomes bored, spends a lot of time doodling and makes very little effort to contribute to the discussion. Your other mentee also struggles to contribute to team meetings but for very different reasons. He lacks confidence and is concerned that his ideas will not be valued by the rest of the team; as a result he tends to sit quietly and contributes only when directly asked to do so.

In theory your mentees have the same issue but for very different reasons, so it would not be appropriate to set them exactly the same goal, even though the outcome of 'contributing to team meetings' is something you want them both to achieve. Taking into account the three domains of skill level, personality and complexity, how might you adapt the goals to suit each of the mentees? The 'bored but confident' mentee does not seem to be concerned about contributing to the meeting; she is just not motivated to do so and the level of boredom displayed suggests that allocating a more complex task might be the best approach here. Perhaps you could arrange for her to present one of her ideas to the next meeting? This would give her some control over content and would ensure that she can't simply switch off during the meeting. It would also be an opportunity to show that ideas are a valuable contribution to the team. For the less confident mentee this particular challenge might create a lot of anxiety so the approach here may be to take smaller steps such as setting a goal of making at least one contribution at the next meeting. Although this may still cause some anxiety, it is unlikely to be all-consuming because any pressure will be short lived.

The goals themselves are less important than the overall aim, which is to change behaviours in relation to team meetings. When working with individual mentees it is important to establish what levels of challenge are valued by them. This ensures that goals become a genuinely developmental tool and not simply a tick-box exercise. We all need some challenge in our lives – the key is to find the right amount of challenge.

Figure 8.2 A sprinkling of magic: challenge for growth

A sprinkling of magic

Challenging the professional practice of others has the potential to lead to positive change. As trees may 'challenge' saplings to grow big and strong, so mentors must provide appropriate challenges to ensure that mentees can reach their full potential. Anything less may be inhibiting. By using the tools outlined in this chapter, mentors also help their mentees to recognise the behaviours and thoughts that are faithfully linked to a sense of self. Similarly the process raises awareness of mentors' own stories and establishes steps for desired change.

In this chapter we have explored the impact of challenge and the ways in which structured questioning may form the basis of setting developmental goals. This approach is at the heart of mentoring because it provides the footing for overcoming behaviours that may be inhibiting development. In addition it creates an opportunity to experience things we may not have even imagined possible, tests our abilities and provides us with information about what we are actually capable of. As suggested by T. S. Eliot (n.d.): 'If you aren't in over your head, how do you know how tall you are?'

Suggested further reading

Egan, G. (1998) *The Skilled Helper: A Problem Management Approach to Helping*. Boston, MA: Brooks-Cole.

References

Black, P. and Wiliam, D. (1998) Assessment and Classroom Learning. *Assessment in Education*, 5(1): 7–71.
Egan, G. (1998) *The Skilled Helper: A Problem Management Approach to Helping*. Boston, MA: Brooks-Cole.
Eliot, T. S. (n.d.) T. S. Eliot Quotes. Available at: https://www.goodreads.com/quotes/32085-if-you-aren-t-in-over-your-head-how-do-you [date accessed 2 August 2018]
Gorzelak, M. A., Asay, A. K., Pickles, B. J. and Simard, S. W. (2015) Inter-Plant Communication through Mycorrhizal Networks Mediates Complex Adaptive Behaviour in Plan Communities. *AoB PLANTS*, (7). 10.1093/aobpla/plv050.

Locke, E. A. and Latham, G. P. (1990) *A Theory of Goal Setting and Task Performance*. Englewood Cliffs, NJ: Prentice Hall.

Yerkes, R. M. and Dodson J. D (1908) The Relation of Strength and Stimulus to Rapidity of Habit Formation. *Journal of Comparative Neurology and Psychology*, 459(18): 482.

9 | Reflection

There is much evidence to suggest that plants are sensitive to their environment and adapt accordingly. They react to change and adopt behaviours to suit their habitat. Plants and trees can adapt to temperature, soil conditions and light in the same way as we adjust to our environment and experiences. Plants, like humans, have developed their senses in ways that allow them to modify behaviours in an attempt to enhance their existence. In the plant world such adaptation is more closely linked to chemical rather than emotional responses, but, in the case of both plant and human species, a process of reflection and learning is the basis of this change.

In this chapter, we explore the ways in which mentors encourage mentees to reflect on their practice, as well as considering how to use those reflections as a springboard for positive change. We review models of reflection and look at some practical strategies for recording and analysing reflections.

The impact of values and assumptions on action

As outlined in Chapter 1, values could be described as the personal 'guidelines' we adopt and as such they influence all aspects of our life such as choices about work, interests, personal relationships and so on. Values are often understood in relation to the things that make up the fabric of existence such as family, peer groups, culture and religion.

They may be evident in societal norms, and witnessed in everyday actions, perhaps made public in the way we dress, interact, work, play and so on. They are also deeply embedded in our life experiences and in this way can be closely linked to the influence of society as a whole. Bourdieu (1984) uses the term 'habitus' to describe the socialised norms or tendencies that guide behaviour and thinking, referring to the way in which certain dispositions and behaviours are determined through society together with other factors that influence our actions, for example the choices we might make because of our interpretation of a certain event. In this way habitus is determined not only by societal structures but also by free will. Although habitus provides us with the skills to successfully traverse social situations, it may also be detrimental if we move into a social scenario that is not governed by the same norms, and one of the mentor's roles is to help mentees to navigate such changes effectively.

Values and beliefs are interconnected; our values could be described as our 'personal truths', representing the things we consider important, for example integrity, courage, fairness and honesty. Our beliefs are the judgements we make about ourselves and the world around us, often based on the things we consider to be true, such as *people are honest/ dishonest, society is fair/unfair* and so on. In turn, both values and beliefs will influence our attitudes and behaviours; they are powerful drivers for the choices we make and the ways we interpret the actions of others. Beliefs grow from our experiences, from the things we see, hear and think, and from these we may develop opinions that we hold to be true, with or without 'evidence' to support them. It could be argued that our beliefs are based on underlying assumptions – things that provide the logic on which to explain a certain principle, for example I have a belief that our society is unfair based on the assumption that individuals do not have equal opportunities. I may have some experiential evidence of this, but it is questionable whether I actually know for certain because I don't know all individuals in all circumstances.

It is possible that our beliefs and the assumptions underlying those beliefs are not correct, or are detrimental to our personal or professional development. Table 9.1 provides some typical examples of such beliefs.

Table 9.1 Examples of beliefs and assumptions

Belief	Assumption
I must behave appropriately at all times	There are appropriate behaviours for given situations
I am not good enough	There is a standard by which we are measured
I must appear professional	Professionalism is recognisable and important
Men (women) are not trustworthy	Gender has an influence on trustworthiness
I am perfect (not perfect)	Perfect exists and is recognisable to everyone

Taking these beliefs at face value it is much easier to see that the assumptions underlying them are not necessarily universal 'truths', but are a reflection of the things we have learnt to believe. As with some of the examples in Table 9.1, it is possible for us to hold on to beliefs that are not useful or limit our potential, and the mentoring relationship provides an opportunity to explore values, beliefs and assumptions in more depth. This is a useful activity, which may help us to implement different behaviours where we feel the need to make changes, and the application of structured reflection is a useful tool in this process.

Models of reflection

Reflective practice could be described as the process of learning from experiences in ways that develop new insights about ourselves and how we work. Through structured reflection we develop self-awareness and critically examine our assumptions and responses to events. The purpose is to recapture experiences and think about them objectively in order to gain new understandings. For anyone in a professional context this is an important activity because the very nature of professionalism is embodied in characteristics such as honesty, integrity and self-regulation.

Reflection can be any activity that causes us to think about experiences in ways that encourage us to question thoughts and actions. It could be as simple as daydreaming or keeping a diary of thoughts and ideas, but if we are to share our reflections with others it may be useful to consider ways of structuring them. That said, this is a very personal activity, so it is important to develop your own approach to it and the following models are offered as suggestions rather than formats to be followed slavishly.

A popular model is that produced by Gibbs (1988), which includes six stages as shown in Figure 9.1.

This model is sometimes described as an iterative model, which means learning through repetition. For this reason the cycle element is important. It is not simply a case of recording an experience but

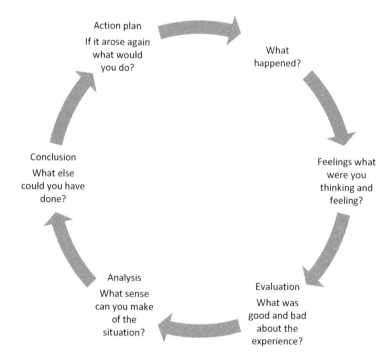

Figure 9.1 Reflective cycle

considering how that experience might be altered by a different approach, which may mean that you actively seek out opportunities to revisit experiences so that you can approach them in a different way. This strategy works well for events that are a regular part of your day-to-day activities, but is less useful when we are reflecting on something that does not have the benefit of frequency.

Petra had recently missed an important deadline at work and this made her feel as if she had let her boss and team members down. She couldn't understand how she could have forgotten something so important and expressed feelings of concern about her abilities. After a brief discussion with you she began to analyse specific aspects of the situation to try to make sense of it. She begins to question whether she simply takes on too much and overloads herself with activities.

Look back at Gibbs' model and identify the various stages in relation to Petra's case. In what ways could you encourage her to address the final two stages of the model? What else could she have done? What potential actions could she take to ensure that this doesn't happen in the future?

In this particular scenario the Gibbs' model works well. Petra has a clear idea of what aspects of the incident she would like to change and has an awareness of why the situation developed in the first place and, in such a case, a very structured reflection linked to action would provide a vehicle for positive change. But what approach is best in situations that are not so simple?

In the following meetings with Petra you notice a pattern in how she is managing her time. After your initial discussion Petra provided examples of success in her time management and expressed feelings of being in control once again, but with time familiar patterns begin to repeat themselves and she reverted to questioning her own abilities by presenting a deficit view of herself. In her view, missing a deadline was not only about letting people down but about 'proving' she wasn't 'good enough' to do the job.

In this scenario, it is unlikely that a very structured model, such as that presented by Gibbs, is likely to bring about any useful understanding. Single incidents that have clear explanations can easily be improved by changing specific aspects of behaviour; however, repeating patterns suggest something that requires deeper reflection to enhance understanding of why patterns are repeating. By gaining an understanding at this level, it is possible to determine what specifically Petra is doing to reinforce the patterns before any strategies are considered.

According to Bolton (2001), reflective practice may be enhanced by becoming as reflexively aware as possible. This means reflecting on yourself as well as a given incident in order to establish the impact your patterns of thought and behaviour have on the incident, as well as your response to it. In a way it is about 'looping back' in order to establish potential actions that are rooted in deeper understanding. This can be done by developing a mindful approach, giving careful consideration to the complexity of situations, rather than simply recording objective observations. Bolton suggests using a *through the looking glass* model which is based on three foundations:

1. Certain uncertainty
2. Serious playfulness
3. Unquestioning questioning.

In a standard reflective model it is possible that you may establish actions before you are clear about why a particular event occurred, so the goals you set yourself might be based on limited information. By taking a *through the looking glass* approach we are not looking for simple answers, but are accepting the notion of certain uncertainty, which recognises that the only thing that is really certain is that we can never really have certainty! Acceptance of this point negates notions of knowing the answer at any given time, something that can be very uncomfortable for mentees who are reflecting in order to seek specific solutions to issues or concerns. Bolton argues that the only way to make sense of this is by adopting *serious playfulness* which means being willing to try out a range of things rather than seeking a specific answer. Within this, *unquestioning questioning* provides an opportunity to generate new meaning and abandon previously held 'truths'.

In a way this is about developing a heightened sense of curiosity whereby you are open to new ideas and possibilities, and develop a tendency to look beyond what is obvious to encourage a 'deep' as opposed to a 'surface' approach to learning. Deep learning is seen as that which requires higher-order cognitive skills and involves analysing and synthesising information to deepen understanding. In contrast, surface learning is acceptance of information that can be memorised for a given purpose (Marton and Säljö 1984). As in Alice's adventures, being curious (and curiouser) adds a new dimension to your learning and your life: there are always new things to attract the attention and new ideas to play with.

Developing reflexivity is something that does not always come easily to mentees, so initial questions linked to a particular reflection might be a useful starting point:

- What was I thinking and feeling?
- What assumptions am I making?
- How do my beliefs and experiences influence my reflections?
- How might this influence my analysis?
- How does this influence my choices about specific actions?

Less structured approaches to reflection can be very powerful tools in generating a range of options, which in turn can be transformative, but it is also worth considering potential pitfalls in this and other forms of reflective practice.

Using reflection to enhance understanding of personal or professional concerns can be a liberating and very helpful in gaining enhanced understanding. In your reflections, you may be considering the actions of others but it is important that the focus is on you; reflection is about improving your understanding of your thoughts, behaviours and actions, not about making judgements about others. It should also be acknowledged that the process of reflection can have an intense emotional impact on the person reflecting, so it does have the potential to be harmful. Brookfield refers to it as laying down psychological dynamite:

> Questioning the assumptions on which we act and exploring alternative ideas are not only difficult but also psychologically explosive.
>
> (Brookfield 1990:178)

The nature of reflection does lead us to strive for constant improvement and this contains the inherent danger of self-flagellation and a potentially negative frame of mind. Therefore, it is imperative to remember the key principle of objectivity and note that criticality, in the form of purposeful thinking, does not necessarily mean criticising. It is also important to ensure that the process is contextualised with a clear purpose and does not simply become a form of egocentric naval gazing. Whichever approach your mentee chooses to adopt, it is important that you help them to reflect in ways that will allow them to gain understanding and develop strategies that will help them in the future.

Ways of recording reflection

To increase the effectiveness of reflection, it is useful to discuss the ways in which reflection can be employed to improve practice. For some mentees this may mean going back to basics and thinking about the sorts of things they might reflect on, with the caveat that this represents only a starter for their reflective practice. Ultimately, personal reflection must be generated by mentees themselves, rather than being overly guided by the mentor. If your mentee is struggling to start this process you might suggest the following as initial reflections:

- Being unprepared to deal with a problem that arose
- Thinking about an event that caused a disturbance of equilibrium
- Discussing a personal or professional dilemma
- Considering actions that seem to have led to a lasting change in professional behaviour, principles or perceptions.

In truth, reflection can be about anything that causes us to think, so it is important to create a sense of openness in relation to topics for consideration.

A further consideration is the strategy your mentee will use to record their reflections. Although it is entirely possible to keep information in their heads, this is less likely to be successful as the passing of time may fade some very important details. There are numerous ways in which reflections can be recorded and the important thing is to select something that is appealing as well as being easy. If your mentee enjoys the process of writing then finding a nice journal that they can carry around with them will help them to jot down thoughts whenever they feel inspired; if they prefer images, something like a mind-map might work well; if they find it difficult to get started then a template adapted from one of the reflective models might be useful.

The format doesn't matter but the ability to reflect honestly and regularly will determine how successful this activity will be, so finding a strategy that works for the individual is essential.

Questions for reflection

A mentor's role in aiding reflective practice is often based around the use of questions that will encourage thinking at a deeper level. These could be based on a Socratic approach, outlined in Chapter 6, or some of the questions presented in the skilled helper model (Egan 1998), which is covered in Chapter 8. Alternatively you could begin with some simple reflective questions to start the process, for example:

- What went well/not so well this week?
- Is there anything you would like to have done differently?
- What has made you curious?
- Is there anything you would like to know more about?

An alternative to questioning would be to present some ideas as a prompt for discussion. These are intended to encourage thinking about beliefs and assumptions and generate discussion on different ways of being. In neurolinguistic programming (NLP) there are a number of presuppositions or tacit understandings that underpin the overall philosophy:

- The map is not the territory.
- The meaning of your communication is the response you get.
- There is no such thing as failure – only feedback.
- Behind every behaviour there is a positive intention.
- All behaviour is communication.
- Those who are flexible have the most influence.
- If you do what you've always done – you get what you always got.
- We are all parts of a system.
- Everyone makes the best choices available to them at the time.
- Our reality is only what we believe to be true.
- We have all the resources we need to succeed or we can create them.

No 'translations' have been offered here because that would only serve to influence discussion. The point of using the presuppositions is to create a starting point for open communication and, if this communication is to be linked to your mentee's reflections, it is important that they are in control of it rather than you. In my experience these work well as practical resources and I have in the past produced a set of cards that simply include one of the statements, which may be presented to individuals or groups as a prompt for further discussion.

Reframing

One of the main aims of reflection is to highlight potential areas for developmental change, and as outlined at the beginning of this chapter this may also mean giving detailed thought to the influence of our beliefs and assumptions on the behaviour choices we make. As individuals we have a tendency to order things into mental 'pigeon holes' as a logical way of making sense of the information we receive; these well-rehearsed, habitual thoughts and understandings are termed 'frames of reference'. A frame of reference is based on a complex set of assumptions through which we might filter our experiences in order to create meaning out of them; as such it has a strong influence on our understanding of and actions in given situations.

Although framing may be useful in helping to construct understanding it is important to remember that we can get 'stuck' in certain ways of thinking and as a result can miss out on new ways of solving problems. It could be argued that the meaning of any event depends on the frame in which we perceive it.

Developing greater awareness of the ways in which we frame events is part of building our emotional intelligence and understanding our natural behaviours. Just as we learn to do very practical things almost without thinking, we also tend to learn behaviours and approaches that manifest themselves in given situations. When you are driving a car or riding a bike, do you think about the sequence of actions you will follow, or do you simply carry out the activity with a degree of unconscious competence? Likewise, when you take part in a meeting at work, or a social gathering, do you think through what you will say and how you will say it, how many times and to whom, or do you tend to conduct yourself in a way that represents a well-rehearsed pattern of behaviours? These activities are framed in a certain way for each of us, and our frames of reference in relation to them are generally so deeply engrained that we often do not even realise we have them until we begin to analyse patterns and behaviours.

Frames of reference can be both positive and negative, for example you may be someone who genuinely sees criticism as feedback that helps you to improve what you do. In this way, your response to criticism will be to value it as something you can utilise to improve your understanding or practice. Alternatively, you may view criticism as a personal insult, in which case the way you respond to it is more likely to be emotional rather than rational. Our frames provide a structure to our experience and when they are firmly set can limit us from achieving what we want and from living life to the full.

Recognising and analysing frames of reference can be a very powerful activity in mentoring and, according to Mezirow (1997), our frames of reference can be not only changed but also transformative. When this is the case it usually involves reframing our thoughts to achieve a different perspective.

Reframing is one method for mentors to aid the process of change, particularly if a mentee appears to be stuck in a way of thinking about things. It enables the introduction of alternative approaches, which in turn offers us choice and flexibility. There are two different types of reframes that we might employ: context reframes and content/meaning reframes.

Context reframes are where we might think about another context in which a given behaviour might seem positive or useful or in what situation this behaviour might be a resource. For example a rebellious co-worker might consistently present objections in meetings; in the initial context this behaviour could be seen as challenging and time-consuming; however, in a different context, such as an explorative working group, this might be useful as the objections might present options or plant seeds for new ideas.

Alternatively, *content/meaning reframes* are relevant when you notice that the mentee is giving a specific meaning to the content they are describing. This could include *presupposition thinking*, for example 'this' happened so it must mean 'this', or *mind reading*:

'They think I am ....' To counteract this, you might offer alternative meanings for the content, for example:

- What else could this mean?
- How else could you describe this situation?
- What is the positive value of this behaviour?
- Is there a larger frame in which this behaviour would have a positive value?

> Evan tells you that his boss has a habit of highlighting his faults in front of the rest of the team and it reminds him of how his mother used make fun of all the 'silly' things he used to do as a child.
>
> It is like being seven years old all over again; my boss will say things like, look at Evan, he isn't afraid of making mistakes, he just goes for it. Or she will give a detailed account of something I have done and have a little laugh about the elements that didn't go so well. I don't mean to say that she is unkind or wants to make me feel bad, I suspect that isn't the case but it is like she has the memory of an elephant when it comes to my mistakes ... all I hear is Evan this, Evan that. I despair!

It is possible that Evan's boss really does enjoy laughing at his mistakes and as you are not involved in these interactions you can only accept his view of events, but taking an objective stance, what else could this mean? It is possible that she is frustrated that most of the team are playing safe and wants to hold him up as an example of good practice because he tries new things? Could it be that Evan's boss wants to create a culture in which people are open and honest about their successes and failures, so she highlights mistakes to show that it is OK to get things wrong? It could also be that she values Evan's contributions to the team and sees this as a way of giving him credit?

The value in reframing is that you can introduce other ways of looking at situations. Although there may be some similarities between Evan's boss and his mother, they are not the same and it is unlikely that their actions are inspired by the same beliefs. By reframing these situations Evan will be able to separate the two and see his boss's actions in a more objective way.

One important consideration is that reframing is about creating the environment in which the mentee can explore potential new understandings. It is not about pushing forward your own frames, it is about allowing others to create or expand their own. It is also important to understand that reframing isn't about taking a rosy view that everything is wonderful and you simply need to think about it differently. Creating a

Figure 9.2 A sprinkling of magic: reflective practice

reframe might actually be the starting point for making significant changes, which inevitably involves work and needs to be thought through carefully in order to find a new frame that fits as neatly as the original one.

A sprinkling of magic

Reflecting on our practice can be a challenging activity and one that stretches mentors and mentees alike. For many mentors, formal reflection is something that they may have been obliged to do during their own professional training but didn't pursue once they were qualified, and yet it is an activity that has the potential to transform thinking and actions.

In the same way that plant life learns to adapt to its habitat, mentors and mentees need to adjust to their own environment and experiences by using reflective practice to develop their understanding and enhance their interactions. The process of mentoring allows mentors to be reflexive in ways that may help adjust unhelpful frames of reference, an opportunity that is far less likely to occur outside of the mentoring relationship.

In this chapter we have explored the benefits of reflection and its potential to generate deeper understandings in order to adapt practice. This process allows us to move beyond habitual, and sometimes unhelpful patterns and can genuinely be a transformative experience; as suggested by Alice: 'I can't go back to yesterday because I was a different person then' (*Alice in Wonderland* cited in guardian.com).

Suggested further reading

Bolton, G. (2001) *Reflective Practice, Writing and Professional Development*. London: Paul Chapman Publishing Ltd.

References

Bolton, G. (2001) *Reflective Practice, Writing and Professional Development*. London: Paul Chapman Publishing Ltd.

Brookfield, S. D. (1990) Using Critical Incidents to Explore Learners' Assumptions. In Mezirow, J. (ed.), *Fostering Critical Reflection in Adulthood*. San Francisco, CA: Jossey-Bass, pp. 177–193.

Bourdieu, P. (1984) *Distinction: A Social Critique of the Judgement of Taste*. London: Routledge.

Egan, G. (1998) *The Skilled Helper: A Problem Management Approach to Helping*. Boston, MA: Brooks-Cole.

Gibbs, G. (1988) *Learning by Doing, A Guide to Teaching and Learning*. London: Longman.

guardian.com. Off with Their Heads, the 10 Greatest Quotes from Alice in Wonderland. Available at: https://www.theguardian.com/childrens-books-site/2015/apr/04/off-with-their-heads-the-10-greatest-quotes-from-alice-in-wonderland [date accessed 25 June 2018]

Marton, F. and Säljö, R. (1984) Approaches to Learning. In Marton, F., Hounsell, D. and Entwistle, N. (eds), *The Experience of Learning*. Edinburgh: Scottish Academic Press.

Mezirow, J. (1997) *Transformative Dimensions of Adult Learning*. San Francisco, CA: Jossey-Bass.

10 Flexibility

If you have ever observed a palm tree in a storm you will notice how much it sways and bends but is rarely uprooted. Palms have short roots which are spread out around them, making a very stable anchor, and their leaves adapt to the climate: in the sun they open out like a fan to offer shade, in heavy rain they close up providing less resistance to the elements, and the shape of their wiry body bends and adapts to their terrain, making them the masters of flexible species.

In this chapter, we explore the importance of taking a flexible approach and consider ways in which mentors help mentees to adapt their thoughts and behaviours in specific situations. This includes raising awareness of current patterns alongside the use of specific strategies to support change.

The importance of a flexible approach

According to Lakoff and Johnson (2003) the concepts governing our thoughts are not purely linked to intellect, they impact on what we perceive, how we manage our activities and how we relate to others. In fact our norms of thinking influence every aspect of our lives. The theory of narrative identity, outlined in Chapter 2, suggests that we internalise such thoughts in the form of 'stories', which help us to build a sense of self and through this accepted identity we convey ourselves to others. Often the ways in which we do this are well rehearsed and become automatic, rather than thoughtful responses which may or may not serve to enhance a given situation, as illustrated in the story in the box:

An armada of the US Navy was engaged in naval exercises off the coast of Canada when the following radio exchange was recorded:

1. 'Please divert your course 15 degrees to the north to avoid danger of collision.'

2. 'Recommend that you divert *your* course 15 degrees to the south to avoid danger of collision.'

1. 'We repeat. Divert north now to avoid collision.'

2. 'Strongly recommend you divert south soonest to avoid mishap.'

1. 'This is the Captain of a US Navy warship. I say again, divert your course with immediate effect.'

2. 'Copy. We say divert south now.'

1. *'This is the USS Enterprise. We are an aircraft carrier of the US Navy. Divert your course NOW!'*

2. 'We are a Canadian lighthouse. Your call!'

(Owen 2001)

Clearly both parties in this story had limited flexibility in their approach to others, or it would seem the flexibility necessary for effective communication! The notion of behavioural flexibility recognises that we all have predominant behaviours and ways of conveying ourselves to others that might be described as personality or personal traits. Sometimes people are depicted in relation to the key characteristics they display to others, such as 'He is a charmer', or 'She's a go-getter' but these rarely describe the person accurately, they are merely a representation of other's perceptions based on typical observed behaviours and probably some assumptions. In a sense this is not that important, particularly when we recognise that perceptions are often based on the things we are allowing others to see; the main problem is that it is easy to get comfortable with common behaviours sometimes making it difficult to do or think about things differently, and this can limit our ability to achieve our overall aims.

In Chapter 9 we considered a range of neurolinguistic programming (NLP) presuppositions that might form the basis of discussion with our mentees when we want to get them to reflect on their actions in constructive ways. The purpose of using these as a tool is to encourage analysis of actions at the same time as considering potential options, and different ways of doing or thinking about things. One of those pre-suppositions is 'All behaviour is communication', which suggests that the image others have of us is not only based on their own perceptions of given scenarios but also on the behaviours we might be exhibiting.

Jennifer sees herself as an efficient and pro-active manager. She manages a very diverse team of people, who have equally diverse approaches to their work and she is trying very hard to get some consistency in the overall department. Jennifer's approach is to put in place what she views as a strong framework of processes for activities, which she further supports by clear monitoring of activity among the team. Some members of the team respond well to this, others don't – so Jennifer puts in place further reinforcements and monitoring in relation to new processes; in response, some members of the team respond as they did before, but others become even more divergent in their application of the new procedures.

Jennifer seems to have a very clear focus: she has a vision for how she wants her department to run and has approached the implementation of this vision with a certain amount of vigour – yet, it isn't working in the way she had envisaged. What questions might you ask Jennifer in order to prompt thinking about her own behaviours and their impact? You might consider questions that allow her to reflect on the effect of her actions, for example, 'What has gone well/less well in relation to the implementation of the new systems?', 'How do the team view the new processes? Do all of the team have the same view?', 'How else might they be interpreting your approach to implementing the new processes?'. Using the underpinning presupposition of 'all behaviour is communication', you encourage Jennifer to think about what message she might be giving her team through her actions; this, in turn, leads to one of the other presuppositions outlined in the previous chapter: 'The meaning of your communication is the response you get.'

Behavioural flexibility is about modifying our own behaviour in order to get the outcomes we want. This doesn't mean doing the same things more often or in a more definite way, it means adopting different approaches that might better suit the context. This allows us to elicit a more desirable response from others and ultimately achieve our outcomes and, as suggested in Chapter 9, 'Those who are flexible have the most influence'.

Recognising and adapting behaviours

Some of the strategies already outlined in this book will help mentees to recognise the thoughts and behaviours that may be limiting them. Usually this process involves structured reflective practice, alongside open and honest communication between mentor and mentee. It is about raising awareness and acknowledging specific thoughts and behaviours that do not support our aims, and we may need to employ a range of strategies in order to develop our awareness. Keeping a reflective journal is a very useful start but this may also be limited by our current patterns. We may have previously kept a journal for a different reason, such as a requirement for a course of study, and adopt the same approach, use the same format or even write the same things. If this is the case it is doubtful that the journal will help us to discover anything we don't already know. Some potential changes could be implemented through trying out different approaches to keeping a journal such as:

- Using journal prompts: this could be a series of interesting quotes that you choose to reflect on, or something like the pre-suppositions outlined in the previous chapter
- Using bullet points rather than discursive writing
- Including images: either your own drawings or a collection of things cut out from magazines
- Stream of consciousness writing: simply writing things as they come into our thoughts without worrying about whether or not it makes sense. This is described by James (cited in Stevenson 2014, p. 39) as: 'nothing joined; it flows. A "river" or a "stream" is the metaphors by which it is most naturally described.'

Each of these will provide a different form of reflection and might be worth trying if the current approach becomes stagnant.

It is also appropriate to use a shared methodology for reflection through the use of cooperative inquiry (Heron and Reason n.d.). Cooperative inquiry involves working with others who may have similar interests or concerns in order to make sense of things and learn how to make useful changes.

Heron and Reason (n.d.) describe this approach as transformative in that it provides the impetus for individuals to 'change their way of being, doing and relating in their world – in the direction of greater flourishing.' (Heron and Reason n.d.) A cooperative inquiry cycle goes through four phases:

1. Phase 1: agree a focus and develop questions/ideas to investigate, then plan a method for investigation through practice experience alongside agreed procedures for gathering and recording data.
2. Phase 2: co-researchers also become co-subjects and observe and record outcomes of their own and each other's actions and experiences.

3. Phase 3: researchers become fully immersed in the experience. At this stage they are open to any preconceptions, have the potential for creative insights and may wish to move away from the original idea into new areas. At this stage, there is a danger of becoming so enthralled in the experience that the original purpose of the inquiry is lost.

4. Phase 4: after the agreed period for the other phases, researchers reassemble to share their experiential data and consider the original ideas in the light of it. As a result they may develop or reframe the ideas and potentially pose new questions which can be explored in a new cycle.

Reluctant reflection

Thinking about our skills, thoughts and behaviours is not something we all find easy to do. There may be many factors that influence a mentee's attitude towards this including prior experiences or previous training and it can be very challenging working with a mentee who does not see the significance of analysing their practice in order to improve it.

> Barry is a trainee teacher undertaking a teaching placement in a local school. Before taking up this opportunity Barry had spent 20 years in the military and still describes himself as an 'ex-soldier'. As part of his placement activities, Barry's mentor suggests that he keeps a reflective journal and he willingly obliges. However, when he shares some of the content of his journal his mentor realises that Barry is actually keeping a factual log of activities including specific details and timing of events. Barry makes no mention of his thoughts and feelings, nor does he attempt to reflect on what he could have done differently. When his mentor makes a suggestion that these might be useful activities he begins to look uncomfortable and finally explains that his experience has taught him to remain completely

objective so that he can follow instructions. After spending 20 years in and environment that does not encourage more subjective thought Barry is finding it very difficult to think about his thoughts, feelings and actions.

Working with a reluctant reflector can be challenging for mentors because the practice of reflection is a key component of change. In the case of Barry, the reflective process is somewhat alien to his work experience so his mentor must take small steps to encourage meaningful reflection. Some potential strategies would be:

- The mentor sharing appropriate information about their own experiences on placement
- Providing evidence of successful reflection though the use of case studies or examples from previous mentoring relationships
- Organising a 'buddy' system with another mentee(s) so that they can discuss their individual experiences
- The use of metaphors to highlight the benefits of thoughtful change
- Temporary use of a journal template which includes space to record thoughts, feelings and potential modifications.

The most important factor is that reflection takes place. With further discussion, patience and guidance, it will then be possible to improve the quality of reflection to ensure that it becomes a springboard for positive change.

'Unfreezing' and generating options

Our state of mind has a significant influence on our thoughts and behaviours and is a powerful manipulator of actions that lead to success or failure in a given situation. Just think about times when you have been in a positive, or resourceful state and almost floated through a day that may have been littered with issues, happily riding along a successful wave of positivity. Conversely, you may also have experienced a negative state whereby your focus is on all of the problems that life is presenting, which in turn can mean that a day that runs relatively smoothly is seen as extremely challenging and every small inconvenience seems to become another mountain to climb.

Although we don't necessarily have control over our emotions in such a way as to choose our state of mind at a given point, we can have a significant influence over them. Demonstrating this to mentees will help them to develop more resourceful approaches to generating options for alternative action. One key to having more control over our state is to develop our awareness of how it impacts on our actions and much of the content of the last two chapters has focused on ways to do this. A second step is to recognise that states can be broken by consciously directing focus elsewhere, so, in the case of a negative state, rather than focussing on things that continue to make us feel negative, switch the focus to something inspiring.

Anchoring

Advocates of NLP would argue that you can actually choose your emotional state by using a technique called 'anchoring'. This works on the premise of redirecting focus by using triggers and normally involves a word or gesture used as an anchor to a particular emotion.

Anchoring is said to create a psychological connection between the trigger (anchor) and an emotional state. To use this technique you would decide on a particular emotional state you wanted to generate, for example being calm, and start by remembering or imagining a situation where you experienced this emotion, trying to make the imagery as vivid as possible, then follow these steps:

* When the imagery of your calm state is vivid enough, use a physiological marker that you want to associate with this state. This could be pressing your thumb and little finger together,

tugging on your ear or stretching out the fingers on your right hand. It doesn't really matter what the action is so long as it is easy to do and something you will remember.

- The next step is to break the state by counting down from ten and then distracting yourself with something else.
- Then apply the anchor again to see if it brings back the calm state. If it doesn't repeat the first steps again.

This strategy might work in the same way as a breathing technique because both are strategies for switching focus from one particular state to another.

The worry decision tree

Mentees who are new to their professional roles may also become so absorbed by perceived issues and concerns that they are unable to switch to more positive states easily so it may be useful to employ some specific strategies to help them do this. The Worry Decision Tree provides a structure for directing attention to pragmatic strategies and helps to focus energies on things that we can do something about. (Butler and Hope 2007; cited in Thompson and Wolstencroft 2018) The technique involves noting anything that is causing concern and then asking the following questions:

- Is there anything I can do about this? If the answer to this is 'yes' – find out what to do and make a list. If the answer is 'no', stop worrying and distract yourself.
- Next, ask yourself if there is anything you can do right now. If the answer is 'yes' then write it down and do it now. Then stop worrying and distract yourself. If the answer is 'no' – plan what you could do and when. Then stop worrying and distract yourself.

This very simple idea is illustrated further in Figure 10.1.

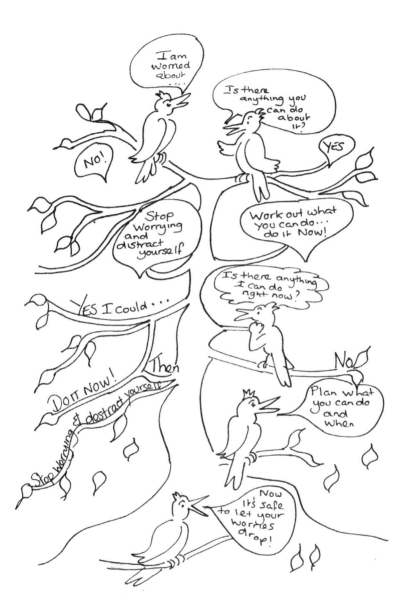

Figure 10.1 The worry decision tree

The worry decision tree provides a tool that can help re-focus thoughts on to potential change, readying the mind for seeking solutions to any issues and concerns. This could be accompanied by a four step approach to problem solving, provided by Butler and Hope (2007:69):

1. Do not waste time on problems that cannot be solved: shift your focus.
2. Tackle one problem at a time.
3. Work on changing yourself, not on changing others.
4. Consider doing nothing, at least for the time being.

Unfreezing, changing and refreezing

Lewin's (1958) change model is based on the analogy of melting a block of ice which can be reshaped into a different form, then 'refreezing' it so that the new change is set in place. Although based on organisational change, this model can also be helpful in mentoring when adaptations are required to enhance a mentee's success. The three stages of the model are, *unfreeze, change* and *refreeze*. The first stage links to motivation for change and relates to readiness to change. If your mentee has demonstrated a repeated pattern that they would like to modify, then discussing this will help to generate ideas about why they wish to change and what potential outcomes they expect from such a change; this analysis of the situation or behaviour is part of the process of *unfreezing*. This is followed by outlining specific strategies that will help implement the required *changes* and putting some of these changes into place. The final *refreeze* stage is about what strategies can be put in place in order to make the change stick, for example, monitoring progress through mentor meetings.

> You have been Farida's mentor for six months and have noticed that she is extremely quiet in team meetings. This is frustrating because she is very chatty when you meet on a one-to-one basis

and often has good ideas that you would like her to share with others. Your concern is that Farida's ideas may go unnoticed, or even worse be credited to someone who is more vociferous in meetings. Initially Farida expressed concern about appearing to be pushy and was very focussed on getting the rest of the team to like her, but after several discussions, Farida has acknowledged that her quietness in meetings may not be helpful to her development. She is now seeking guidance on how she might adapt her behaviour to ensure that her ideas are recognised by the people who may be able to help implement them.

Which of the strategies outlined in this chapter might be useful in helping Farida to change her behaviour in team meetings? How could you encourage her to think differently about putting forward her ideas? How would you ensure that new behaviours become permanent changes?

The approaches outlined in this chapter provide some practical strategies that can be used to support a mentee's development and help create awareness of the need for change as well as highlighting specific strategies to put such changes in place.

A sprinkling of magic

Flexibility is a fundamental aspect of change but, in order to be flexible, we must first be aware. Change for the sake of change is not necessarily a positive and may not lead to the outcomes we want but ecologically sound change, that is change that is grounded in observation, reflection and awareness can have a significant impact on our communication, interaction and personal development.

In the same way that palm trees adapt their form to be more in tune with their habitat, we each need to adjust to the personal and professional contexts we occupy. The mentor's role in supporting the use of more flexible approaches is twofold: in the first instance it requires encouragement towards reflexivity, followed by the need to adjust mentoring practice should the mentee be resistant to reflective

Figure 10.2 A sprinkling of magic: flexibility

activities. In turn this builds mentors' own skills, knowledge and flexible behaviours.

In this chapter we have explored the need for flexibility based on awareness of our thoughts and behaviours and considered how adaptability allows us to implement positive changes. The recognition that change is something we can control is a powerful tool for both mentors and mentees and our ability to reflect openly and honestly is a stepping stone towards providing us with the ability to adapt.

Suggested further reading

Lakoff, G. and Johnson, M. (2003) *Metaphors We Live By*. London: University of Chicago Press.

References

Butler, G. and Hope, T. (2007) *Manage Your Mind, the Mental Fitness Guide* (2nd edn). Oxford: Oxford University Press.

Heron, J. and Reason, P. (n.d.) The Practice of Co-operative Inquiry: Research with Rather than on People (online). Available at: www.peterreason.eu/Papers/Handbook_Co-operative_Inquiry.pdf [date accessed 17 January 2018].

Lakoff, G. and Johnson, M. (2003) *Metaphors We Live By*. London: University of Chicago Press.

Lewin, K. 1958, Group Decision and Social Change, In Maccoby, E. E., Newcomb, T. M. and Hartley, E. L. (eds), *Readings in Social Psychology*. New York: Holt, Rinehart & Winston, pp. 197–211.

Owen, N. (2001) *The Magic of Metaphor, 77 Stories for Teachers, Trainers & Thinkers*. Carmarthen: Crown House Publishing Ltd.

Stevenson, R. W. (2014) *Modernist Fiction: An Introduction* (revised edn). Oxon: Routledge.

Thompson, C. and Wolstencroft, P. (2018) *The Trainee Teachers' Handbook: A Companion for Initial Teacher Training*. London: Learning Matters.

Mentoring
creativities

What do you see in a tree? Something purely ornamental, a form of protection or an integral part of the environment? Trees have been portrayed in many ways; in history they represent knowledge, life, growth and connection. In the garden of Eden the tree of knowledge symbolised wisdom and temptation; in mythology trees are seen as embodying deities or are believed to be humans in tree form. The Tree of Life depicted within myths provides us with a mystical notion representing the interconnectedness of all things.

This powerful embodiment of nature has its roots deeply embedded in the earth and its crown stretching towards 'heaven'. Gustav Klimt's famous painting of the same name draws the eye to an abundance of twists and turns, representing life's often circuitous route, and the tree reaches towards the sky which is said to represent man's eternal quest to be more than he currently is, while at the same time recognising that his roots are firmly fixed to the earth (see https://www.gustav-klimt.com/The-Tree-Of-Life.jsp). Trees can be seen as the embodiment of creativity, providing so much to so many, inspiring art in many forms and representing life, knowledge and growth in so many cultures.

In this chapter, we explore the potential boundaries to creativity and consider ways of overcoming these by adopting creative mentoring strategies. We also look at some simple techniques that can be used to enhance creative thought.

The glass box

In Chapter 9 we considered the idea of 'frames of reference' (Mezirow 1997) and their influence on our thoughts and actions. This notion is developed further by Goffman (1974) who outlines the practice of configuring our experiences in ways that make sense, a process that can include filtering important information in the construction of our perception of 'reality'. Such framing provides a way of explaining what is going on for us and which bits of that experience are relevant to our personal representation of the world. Goffman suggests that humans don't consciously create these life frames but unconsciously adopt them according to their understanding of a situation, which in turn guides future action, a form of cognitive organisation of social encounters. Similarly, O'Brien (2011) makes reference to how we create boundaries of meaning by framing various realms of experience. In this way we are separating the 'ordinary' aspects of day-to-day existence from the world of art, play or symbolism and the metaphorical from the literal. This activity has the benefit of helping us to contain events within frameworks we understand, but can also be very limiting and keep us within tightly confined mental glass boxes looking out at the world. When we try to move to another mental space we bump into the glass walls and are made more aware of the existence of our own prisons (Zerubavel, cited in Bell 1992). The confines of our own minds have a powerful influence on all aspects of life and drawing once again on the work of Korzybski (1933), we sometimes need reminding that 'The map is not the territory' and the way we currently see the world isn't necessarily 'reality'.

Breaking the metaphorical glass box is a complex activity, particularly when it contains long-held beliefs about what is and isn't true for us. In mentoring this situation is further complicated by a scenario in which both parties have individual perceptions, yet must create a platform that allows exploration of alternative views. In any environment these limitations provide a very real constraint for variance from the norm and, more specifically, the divergent thinking usually associated with creativity. It could be argued that significant aspects of western culture, such as education, also have a negative impact on our ability to think creatively; this belief is articulated clearly in a quote often attributed to Picasso: 'all children are artists, the problem is staying an artist when you grow up.' (Pablo Picasso Quotes online 2018). According to Ken Robinson this is a situation that needs to be addressed if we hope to grow creative potential within society, suggesting that we should learn to 'think differently about our talents and abilities' (Robinson 2017:5), an opinion supported by Samples (1976) who puts forward the view that society has a strong focus on rationality and asserts that: 'The metaphoric mind is a maverick. It is as wild and unruly as a child. It follows us doggedly and plagues us with its presence as we wander the contrived corridors of rationality' and quoting Einstein he suggests that, by ignoring that which is not considered rational, we may be limiting our potential:

> Einstein called the intuitive or metaphoric mind a sacred gift. He added that the rational mind was a faithful servant. It is paradoxical that in the context of modern life we have begun to worship the servant and defile the divine.
>
> (Samples 1976:26)

Your mentee seems to have very definite ideas about how things *are*, or *should* be. Recently she described an incident where she was passed over for a promotion in favour of another person in the department. In your mentee's view, she has been in post the longest and *must* have the most experience; she is also very definite about what she sees as protocol within the organisation, which is that the person who has worked in the department the longest should be the first in line when a promotion comes up. Instead, a relative newcomer, who has only worked in the team for six months, was offered the post. Your mentee is complaining bitterly about this and says this is *definitely* a sign that she is being bullied by her boss, who didn't recommend her for the promotion that was *rightly* hers.

What is going on for this mentee? How might her frame of reference be hindering her progress? This is a clear example of someone being trapped by their way of thinking rather than being able to think differently about a situation; it also illustrates how deeply engrained beliefs about what is and should be are having a negative impact, particularly if accusations of bullying are being voiced elsewhere. In this scenario it would be useful to get your mentee to try to think differently about the situation both in terms of accommodating the information that she is not getting the hoped for promotion and in seeking strategies for positive change.

When we are faced with mentees who do not respond to the usual mentoring strategies, such as questioning and reflective discussion, it might be useful to try out different methods that may help focus thinking in a new direction and encourage thoughts and actions that may have a more positive outcome.

Insights through focused reflection

As outlined in Chapter 9, the process of reflection helps us to generate new insights. When our ability to think creatively is limited by our perceptions we may need to take more focused approaches in order to produce alternatives. One method of reflection that helps us to address an issue from a number of perspectives is the critical lens approach, originally developed to help teachers reflect on their practice (Brookfield 1995). In this model Brookfield suggests that we can encourage greater awareness by critically analysing a situation from four different perspectives:

1. The autobiographical: refers to our own current or historical experiences in a given scenario and represents the 'felt' aspect of an event.

2. The students/other participants' eyes: considers how other participants might have viewed the particular incident.

3. Colleagues' views/experiences: encourages us to think about what colleagues made of the incident.

4. Theoretical literature: examines what the literature says – are there any theories that might explain the event?

By taking this very structured approach to reflection we are not limiting ourselves to our own perception or even to our initial emotional response to a particular situation. Viewing something through a range of lenses offers information from different perspectives and may allow us to see things differently, subsequently influencing any further thoughts and actions.

Creative thinking

Creativity is a term often associated with a 'special few' who have the ability to produce great works of art, but this may be a misconception. We could argue that everyone can take creative approaches to day-to-day activities; think about the way a barista might fashion an interesting image in your coffee, how a cook might arrange food on a plate, how some people dress, how others present themselves and so on. We all have creative capacities that are probably being utilised in environments not usually associated with the creative arts. As mentors, we may view our role as being the facilitators for our mentees' creativity but we should also remember that, in order to do this, the likelihood is that we will have to adopt more creative methods ourselves, sometimes bypassing the usual approach to mentor–mentee interactions. This could be described as a pragmatic approach to being creative, 'Creativity involves putting your imagination to work. In a sense, creativity is applied imagination' (Robinson 2017:121).

The magic of curiosity

According to Gilbert (2015) creativity is a form of magic and the ideas that form part of the creative process are disembodied energy, completely separate from us but able to interact with us. In Gilbert's view, ideas are driven by the impulse to be known and can only do this through human interaction, so we might be 'visited' by ideas that we choose to work with or not. In her view, most people say 'no' to ideas, so they must then visit the next likely candidate in order to reach their ultimate aim. What can we do if we want to encourage such visitations? One strategy might be to cultivate our curiosity. For most of us, enhanced curiosity makes us much more open to new possibilities and provides us with the tools to look beyond what is obvious. In this way, we might recognise an idea for what it is rather than just dismissing it as a passing thought. Being curious adds a new dimension to our ability to be creative because there are always things to attract the attention and plenty of new ideas to play with. If you are not a naturally curious person, enhancing your curiosity may take time and practice, but the following pointers may help:

- Have an open mind: what you 'know' now may change
- Ask questions: what, why, when, who, how?
- Avoid labelling things as boring: if something hasn't grabbed you, it may need further exploration
- Learn new things: and have fun so that you enjoy the process
- Make small changes: to your routines, habits, thought patterns
- Don't limit your reading: read widely and look at diverse sources of information.

Bisociation

According to Steve Jobs (Co-founder of Apple Inc.) (1996), creativity is simply a matter of connecting things and in his view creative people can connect experiences they have had in order to synthesise new ideas. This suggests that creativity is more about the ability to 'see' things than generating entirely new concepts, and in its simplest form this means that we need to practise seeing things differently in order to enhance our creative potential.

In formulating a theory about how human creativity transpires, Koestler's classic work (1975) put forward the term 'bisociation' which refers to the combination of an object or idea from two fields that are not normally considered to be related; in effect this is the connection of disparate ideas in order to come up with new approaches. Think about the use of tragedy in comedy creating an almost illicit form of humour, or combining unlikely ingredients such as meat and chocolate to produce a marvellously rich dish.

The term 'bisociation', rather than association, illustrates the autonomous nature of the items brought together, the juxtaposition of two almost incongruent things providing a forum from which to compare, highlight contrasts and synthesise new ideas. This idea was brought into the teaching and learning context by Beadle (2011), who advocates the connection of distinct separates in order to come up with new approaches. He provides an example of this with his approach to teaching punctuation through a series of Kung Fu moves. In this method, punctuation marks such as full stop and semi-colon are attached to a corresponding Kung Fu move with associated sounds and students are taught to demonstrate the punctuation marks in a fun and active way.

Take a look at Table 11.1 and complete the empty space with a single word.

The chances are that your automatic reaction would be to complete this as a word association activity, so probable entries would be something linked to your experience of lemons, the sun and school. If you were to try the activity again on the basis of disassociation you would then be seeking words that bear as little resemblance as possible to the words in the first column, for example as shown in Table 11.2.

If linking together the more disparate items, you would then be seeking new connections between lemon and puppy, sun and snail, school and lawnmower. This of course is far less obvious in terms of connection and requires a more creative approach to make the link.

Table 11.1 Bisociation activity

Lemon	Peel	Sour
Sun	Round	Heat
School	Books	Reading

Table 11.2 Examples of disassociation

Lemon	Peel	Sour	Puppy
Sun	Round	Heat	Snail
School	Books	Reading	Lawnmower

It is a challenge but certainly a strategy that forces us to think differently.

Seven strategies for fostering creativities

Although it is probably difficult to force creative approaches in any activity, it is possible to build environments that support the process. The following ideas may be something you could try with your mentees if you would like to help them to test out alternative methods or to think about things differently. Some may appeal more than others, but it is important to keep an open mind and to remember that when you read this you are approaching it from your own map of reality, which may be very different to your mentee's. With this thought in mind, consider which which strategies may be useful.

Symbolic timeline of life

This activity involves drawing a 'roadmap' of life to date and creates an image of important events, people or objects. In a way it provides a pictorial autobiography and should highlight discussion points that may be helpful in establishing potential options or obstacles. The starting point is to list a number of items that are important, starting from birth. These could be milestones in life, specific events, trips, important people or things. It is useful to list 15–20 items initially, then reconsider the list and select half of those to 'map out'. There are no rules for this activity, other than trying to convey all the information using images rather than words.

Timeline activities are useful in helping us to establish meaningful events in our lives and help us to gain a deeper understanding of our current state and potential direction. It will aid reflection, particularly in relation to repeated patterns of behaviour, and may provide some insights. This in turn helps us think about possible changes and steps we might want to take to implement these.

Scripted fantasy

This is based on a technique employed in teaching social and emotional skills, which involves the use of a short relaxation exercise followed by a series of suggestions that form a framework of the 'fantasy'. The participants are then free to enter the world of their own imagination, taking the fantasy to wherever they see fit (Hall and Leech 1990).

If you have ever been to a meditation or relaxation class you may have come across something similar. The suggestion is that, by adopting a relaxed state and making use of imagery, we are moving away from the domination of more logical thinking and using our imagination to explore thoughts, feelings and ideas.

Mind-mapping

Most people are familiar with Tony Buzan's mind-mapping technique, which has its roots in the belief that the brain is more than the logical information-processing tool it is often described as (Buzan 2010). Instead the human brain is seen as:

> an enchanted loom where millions of flashing shuttles weave a dissolving pattern, always a meaningful pattern, though never an abiding one, a shifting harmony of sub-patterns. It is as if the Milky Way entered upon some cosmic dance.
>
> (Buzan 2010:29)

Mind-maps avoid the use of linear approaches and encourage free-flowing thoughts and the connections between them. The usual technique is to use a large sheet of paper in landscape rather than portrait format and in the middle of this place a central image that captures the main subject under consideration. From this central image thick branches radiate out to represent key themes, each one

Figure 11.1 Chapter mindmap

signified by a different colour. An image or words are placed on each branch, from then on further images and branches are added to represent connected information. An example outlining the content of this chapter has been included in Figure 11.1.

Picture association

Imagery is often linked to our creative capacities because it allows us to both view and depict things in non-linear ways. A strategy that may be useful within the mentoring context is the use of images to prompt discussion or idea generation. There are several sets of ready-made cards you can buy, or you could make a set of your own by collecting, printing and laminating different images. The cards are usually no bigger than A6 because this makes them easy to manipulate. They can be chosen on the basis of things that appeal to the mentee, or a selection could be made to plot out a series of events. Alternatively images could be allocated randomly and used as an idea generator. There are really no rules so long as the activity prompts some sort of discussion.

Six thinking hats

This technique is based on the work of Edward De Bono (2000) and is used as a strategy for generating solutions to problems. The use of the six thinking hats provides a platform to explore issues from a variety of perspectives and forces people to move outside of their normal thinking style. It is ideally suited to group situations, where individuals could adopt a different thinking hat each but this could also be adapted to suit a one to one meeting by switching between hats. The six thinking hats are:

1. The white hat: this considers the 'facts'.
2. The yellow hat symbolises optimism and brightness and explores the positives, seeking out value and benefit.
3. The black hat represents judgement; it could be the devil's advocate and spots dangers, difficulties and where things might go wrong.
4. The red hat signifies feelings and links to intuition. When 'wearing' this hat you can express emotions such as likes, fears, dislikes, love, hate.
5. The green hat has a focus on creativity so it seeks out possibilities, alternatives and new ideas.
6. The blue hat manages the thinking process; it keeps the others under control and ensures that guidelines are followed.

Sandbox

Sandbox or sand-tray activities allow a person to construct his or her own microcosm using miniature objects such as people, animals, trees, houses, etc. and a tray full of sand (Dale and Lyddon

1998). Participants are asked to select a number of items and create a scene within the sand; the scene itself acts as a reflection of the person's own life, providing an opportunity to resolve conflicts, remove obstacles and gain acceptance. There are no right or wrong ways of doing this and often people need little direction. Once the scene has been created ask your mentee what is happening in it; this should prompt meaningful discussion and the opportunity to explore any prominent ideas or concerns. Sandbox activities provide a forum from which to express any potential issues or concerns, as well as try out fledgling ideas and they do not require any artistic ability.

Artefacts

The dictionary definition of artefact refers to something made or given shape by 'man'. In this context it is simply an alternative form of expression. The use of an artefact is a way of inspiring thought and discussion, and can be employed in a number of ways. Mentees could select from a range of items and write down key words that come to mind in relation to these items – or they could compile a selection in order to create a story. An artefact could also be used just as a random thought generator, for example 'How many uses can you think of for this paper clip?'. At first glance this activity does not have an immediate use in relation to exploring issues or finding solutions to problems, but it does encourage us to think in different ways, which may be a stepping stone to becoming 'unstuck'.

Using stories to enhance thinking

Stories have had their place in human society for thousands of years, from the ancient Egyptians who depicted every aspect of life and mythology through their tomb paintings, to the *spin* used by modern PR professionals. In many cultures stories are used to pass on moral tales and reinforce cultural norms as they provide a distinct way of contextualising information. On the one hand, stories can be viewed as an innocuous form of entertainment, and, on the other, a way of providing a clear message that the recipient can personalise to their own experience. We all use stories to make sense out of information and to communicate with others; as a result, this has become a widely accepted method of enhancing learning.

Making use of stories to introduce new information is a valuable tool because it offers a way of personalising this to our own experiences and opens up the potential for new windows of understanding. A story can stir the imagination in ways that other methods cannot. By telling a story we are also painting a picture, the detail of which can be contextualised to make it memorable at an individual level. Stories can challenge us by providing a different perspective and have the power to transform the everyday into the extraordinary if used in the right way. That reminds me of a story.

A group of travellers had been asked to collect pebbles, something they saw as pointless until the pebbles turned into diamonds. When reflecting on their experience, the travellers considered the difference between something they had considered worthless and then extremely valuable. This reflection, when applied in a wider sense, made them wonder how many other things in their lives, which they had considered of little or no consequence, might have a value that they hadn't yet discovered. As a result, they began to get more and more curious about discovering meanings under the surface of things, which only now were they beginning to comprehend (Hodgson 2010).

Stories can be used within the framework of mentor–mentee meetings and as self-study activities used between meetings. You could read one to your mentee to prompt a discussion, or ask them to share a story with you. They are a very useful tool for enhancing reflection, so you could also give your mentee a story to reflect on at the end of a meeting and use this as a starting point for the next meeting. There are a number of sources that include a range of stories for reflection and enhancing learning, so it is worth making a collection of your own to add to your mentoring toolbox.

A sprinkling of magic

The mentor and mentee work together to construct their own type of magic in the form of knowledge, skills and understanding, the development of which could be described as 'the art of transformation

Figure 11.2 A sprinkling of magic: developing creativity

and change' (Owen 2001:xi). Although this is a collective effort, it is also based on the presupposition that the individuals in the relationship bring to it diversity in experience alongside different perceptions. Therefore, a 'one-size-fits-all' approach may not be possible, and for this reason mentors may need to adopt more creative strategies to engage their mentees. In turn, mentees may wish to consider more creative approaches to their professional practice.

In this chapter we have explored the meaning of creativity and the potential barriers to it. In doing so it is acknowledged that creativity is not merely the premise of artists and poets but something we all possess, a fundamental part of human existence. To reinforce this notion, some specific strategies have been proposed which are aimed at enhancing our creative capacities by providing opportunities to change our perspective as, according to De Bono: 'Creativity involves breaking out of established patterns in order to look at things in a different way' (Vliet 2011).

Suggested further reading

Gilbert, E. (2015) *Big Magic, Creative Living Beyond Fear*. London: Bloomsbury.

Robinson, K. (2017) *Out of Our Minds, the Power of being Creative* (3rd edn). London: John Wiley & Sons Ltd.

References

Beadle, P. (2011) *Dancing about Architecture: A Little Book of Creativity* (Independent Thinking Series). Carmarthen: Crown House Publishing.

Bell, J. (1992) Cross Cultural Studies. Paper presented to Teachers Stories of Life and Work Conference, Chester.

Brookfield, S. (1995) *Becoming a Critically Reflective Teacher*. San Francisco, CA: Jossey-Bass.

Buzan, T. (2010) *The Mindmap Book: Unlock Your Creativity, Boost Your Memory, Change Your Life*. Harlow: BBC Active.

Dale, M. A. and Lyddon, W. J. (1998) Sandplay: A Constructivist Strategy for Assessment and Change. *Journal of Constructivist Psychology*, 13(13): 135–154.

De Bono, E. (2000) *Six Thinking Hats*. London: Penguin.

Goffman, E. (1974) *Frame Analysis, an Essay on the Organization of Experience*. London: Harper & Row.

Hall, E. and Leech, A. (1990) *Scripted Fantasy in the Classroom*. London: Routledge.

Hodgson, D. (2010) *Magic of Modern Metaphor, Walking with the Stars*. Carmarthen: Crown House Publishing Ltd.

Jobs, S. (1996) Wired interview. Available at: https://www.brainpickings.org/2011/10/20/i-steve-steve-jobs-in-his-own-words/ [date accessed 14 July 2018].

Koestler, A. (1975) *The Act of Creation*.London: Picador.

Korzybski, A. (1933) *Science and Sanity, an Introduction to Non-Aristotelian Systems and General Semantics*. The International Non-Aristotelian Library Pub. Co. 747–761.

Mezirow, J. (1997) *Transformative Dimensions of Adult Learning* (1991). San Francisco, CA: Jossey-Bass.

O'Brien, J. (2011) *The Production of Reality, Essays and Readings on Social Interaction* (5th edn). Thousand Oaks, CA: Pine Forge Press.

Owen, N. (2001) *The Magic of Metaphor, 77 Stories for Teachers, Trainers and Thinkers*. Carmarthen: Crown House Publishing Ltd.

Pablo Picasso Quotes Online: Available at: https://www.pablopicasso.org/quotes.jsp [date accessed 26 May 2018].

Robinson, K. (2017) *Out of Our Minds, the Power of Being Creative* (3rd edn), London: John Wiley & Sons Ltd.

Samples, B. (1976) *The Metaphoric Mind: A Celebration of Creative Consciousness*. Boston, MA: Addison-Wesley Publishing Co.

12 | Mentoring dilemmas

When a tree is growing well, has firm roots and full branches, it is considered to be healthy. In this state trees enhance our environment by removing contaminants from the air and producing oxygen; they also provide a habitat for birds and other wildlife, give us shade and absorb noise pollution. In addition to this, they add beauty to the world and provide inspiration to artists and environmentalists alike. Trees are generally considered positive inhabitants of the world, but what happens when a healthy tree is blocking other life, perhaps by absorbing the majority of light, or taking up too much space through its roots? In this case, is the best course of action to kill one tree to save another?

We are faced with dilemmas in all aspects of life and although most of those connected to mentoring do not usually relate to life and death situations, they are nevertheless a cause for concern for mentors and mentees alike. In this chapter we explore a range of dilemmas that may occur in mentoring and consider the options available to help resolve these.

Dilemmas in mentoring

According to the *Oxford English Dictionary* a dilemma refers to a difficult situation that normally involves making a choice between options. In mentoring this can range from dilemmas about how best to work with your mentee in order to get the most out of the relationship, to how to help your mentee overcome obstacles to progression. Many of the strategies that may help with these situations are outlined in previous chapters. A second type of dilemma is one that is ethical in nature; this relates to the boundaries in the mentoring relationship outlined in Chapter 3 and usually refers to situations where you feel unable to support your mentee because you are presented with something outside your expertise, or because an aspect of ethics is being challenged. As outlined in Chapter 3, the ethical framework advocated is one that includes the following:

- Being trustworthy
- Providing an environment in which your mentee has the autonomy to be self-governing
- Beneficence based on a commitment to promoting your mentee's wellbeing
- Non-maleficence based on a commitment to avoiding harm, which may include knowing when to refer your mentee to someone else
- Justice, including impartial treatment for all mentees
- Self-respect, fostering your own self-knowledge and care.

Suresh has been working with you for a few months and you have noticed a recurring pattern in his response to problems. Whenever anything goes wrong, or even slightly off-plan, he is highly critical of himself and seems to become completely overwhelmed by negativity. His usual pattern is to get into a panic state and then follow a vicious cycle into despair. This changes his approach to work and to other team members and he sometimes becomes very snappy with colleagues.

Suresh is actually very competent and well liked within the team; he is seen as hard working and innovative, but people are starting to become wary of saying anything to him that might be interpreted as criticism and you are concerned that this may limit his overall development.

You have already discussed aspects of emotional intelligence with him and tried to encourage him to express exactly what is going on when he starts to panic. This had some initial success but Suresh seems to have fallen back into old habits and you now need to consider the best way forward.

In this case, it seems that the mentee is very caught up in how they *think about* their performance, rather than the *actual* performance, and what is required is some sort of perspective change. Based on this premise, is this situation something you could approach in a different way and, if so, what strategies could you use to help move the situation on in a more positive way? Some examples might be:

- Try using the reframing technique outlined in Chapter 9. This is based on the idea that the meaning of any event depends on how we frame it; therefore if we can change the frame, we can change the meaning and subsequently our response to a given event.

- Use targets to practise behaviour changes. This means that you are focusing on one aspect of the dilemma, for example getting snappy with colleagues. By using questions to enhance your mentee's autonomy it is possible to highlight the undesirable behaviour and ask, 'what could you do instead?'.

- Use focused reflection and try to see the situation from different perspectives. One way to structure this would be to use a framework for reflection such as Brookfield's lenses, outlined in Chapter 11. This approach allows your mentee to see the situation from a number of viewpoints and takes the focus away from his own, self-critical analysis.

You have been working with Gordon for a month now and he feels he is making excellent progress both in his new role and in his personal development. He often tells you what a great job he is doing and how everyone in the department has commented on his progress. Feedback from other colleagues suggests otherwise, and you feel that Gordon's narcissistic approach may well be alienating those with whom he works closely.

Gordon's role is one in which he is afforded a large amount of trust. He works very closely with external clients and has access to a lot of personal information. In his meetings with you he often 'let's slip' snippets of information that he thinks you might find interesting, leading to mistrust in your relationship with him.

There are two main concerns for you: one is that Gordon appears to be abusing the trust that is placed in him and the other is that your own feelings towards Gordon are affected by your own lack of trust in him. Added to this, his particular brand of narcissism is something you don't admire, so you have admitted to yourself that you don't actually like him much either!

This is a tricky situation because it involves your own emotional response to your mentee alongside a potential ethical dilemma, so the first decision is whether or not this is something you can deal with on your own or whether you need to involve others. A good starting point to resolving this dilemma is to reconsider the ethical guidelines outlined earlier and think about which ones specifically relate to this situation.

Trustworthiness does seem to be at the root of this particular dilemma and, although this is usually considered in the light of the mentor's trustworthiness to provide the best support, in this case there are clearly issues of trust in relation to the mentee. In relation to beneficence and non-maleficence, a mentor would be faced with a difficult challenge here. It may well be in the best interests of the mentee to try to access the 'truth' of the situation, which may lead to unearthing potential ethical concerns. If this is the case, how does the mentor ensure non-maleficence and at the same time let relevant others know that the mentee may be abusing the trust placed in him?

Finally, it is important to consider self-respect. If you are respecting yourself, this also means acknowledging your feelings towards your mentee, which in turn may be influencing how you are working with him. In this case is the best solution to try to establish the root of the feelings, and potentially overcome them, or to acknowledge them and find a mentor who can provide better support?

A six-step process for ethical dilemmas

According to Clutterbuck (2016) there is a six-step process to working with ethical dilemmas:

1. Articulate the problem
2. Consider the context
3. Consider the implications
4. Think about other opinions/perspectives may be relevant
5. Balance the arguments
6. The final check.

Articulating the problem is a key stage because it provides the foundation from which to work through the concern. It is possible that the mentee in this case is not aware of potential issues, or is ignoring them for some reason they haven't yet shared. In this scenario you may wish to use questions that allow the mentee to highlight the concerns, or their particular perspective. For example:

• What might be the issue with you sharing personal information about clients?
• How might this affect the client or the organisation?
• How might others view this?
• Is there any potential conflict for you or others?

Considering the context provides an opportunity to highlight the scope of the issue and will allow the mentee to think about those outside of her immediate circle. To highlight this you could ask questions such as:

- Who does this directly involve?
- Is there anyone indirectly involved?
- Is there a relevant code of conduct to be followed in this situation?
- What is the potential impact on others in the organisation?

Considering implications is a way of exploring what the impact might be of following one path or another. In this case, what is the impact of your mentee continuing to share confidential information, or the impact of changing his approach? These questions are important for helping to change perspective by considering the bigger picture. You could ask:

- What are the potential risks?
- What is the possible impact of your actions?
- How could you approach this differently?
- If you made that/those changes, what might be the impact?

Considering the opinions of others helps to widen perspective further because it considers the light in which the mentee is, or might be, viewed. There is also the potential that your mentee has not considered the viewpoints of others and in neglecting to do so has formed a very narrow outlook. To elicit information about other perspectives you could ask:

- What might you be avoiding acknowledging?
- Have you considered the views of others in this scenario?
- If you were the (use an appropriate name or label, such as 'client'), how might you feel about this?

Working through the previous steps should have provided more specific information giving sufficient detail to outline the choices available. If appropriate this can then be linked to future actions. Some useful questions at this point might be:

- What are the conflicting objectives and values here?
- What might an impartial adviser consider to be the best action?
- What are the next steps?

The final check is a way of ensuring that any agreed changes are both ethical and in tune with your mentee's values. Some potential questions to include here are:

- What potential biases might be informing your decisions?
- How honest are you being with yourself?
- Do you feel your decision is right?
- Is it likely that in time you might come to a different conclusion?

According to Clutterbuck (2016) one likely outcome of taking an ethical stance is that the other person may respond negatively because their integrity is being questioned, and in this case the instinctive response might be based on resentment or fear. He suggests that to overcome this it is helpful to try to link the conversation to the other person's values or to those of the organisation. The final acknowledgement in this six-step process is that it may not always be possible to establish an ethical way forward and there will be occasions when whistleblowing is the only option. If this is the case, your organisation's policies, your personal values and guidance from other mentors may be helpful in leading you to the right decision.

> Lizzie is a trainee teacher with whom you have been working for the last six months. She is studying at a local university and has her teaching placement in your school. You have worked with the university for several years mentoring trainees and have always found this a rewarding thing to do. This is still very much the case as Lizzie seems to be progressing really well on

her course and her confidence in the classroom seems to go from strength to strength. You have found the whole experience to be very positive, not only because she responds so well to the support you are giving her but also because you are learning a lot from watching her very creative approach to teaching. She is a natural teacher and a joy to observe.

At your last meeting Lizzie was extremely upset and angry. Eventually she told you that she had paid a lot of money for something that would help with her studies, had been let down by the provider and was considering not paying her debt to them. When you dug a little further you discovered that Lizzie had been struggling to manage her time and wanted to focus her attention on preparing for her teaching, so she had been paying an internet company for 'ready-made' essays that would help her through her course. This had been working well up until now but the last essay had not received a very good grade and Lizzie was upset because this would impact on the overall outcome of her training. In her fury, Lizzie was unable to see anything wrong with this scenario other than the fact that she had been cheated.

This dilemma may well be complicated by the relationship you have built up with the mentee and the fact that, in all other aspects, she has been an ideal candidate for mentoring. However, you also have a responsibility to the university, the school and the profession as a whole, and it is clear that a definite boundary has been crossed. Taking into account the ethical guidelines of justice and self-respect, you must consider what actions you would take for any mentee with whom you were working and acknowledge the importance of your role in modelling professional behaviour. That said, there may be ways to encourage Lizzie to take control of this situation, something that may be to her advantage in the long run. The following are some potential strategies:

- Use a Socratic questioning approach (outlined in Chapter 6) to elicit thinking behind choices and actions. Those questions specifically related to questioning perspectives and consequences would be particularly useful here, for example:

- What alternative ways of looking at this are there?
- What is the difference between ... and ...?
- What would ... say about it?
- What are the implications of ...?
- How does ... affect ...?
- How does ... fit with what we learned before?

- Use a metaphor or story to put the mentee in your situation and ask them to consider what they might do if faced with this dilemma

- Involve others in the support network, for example the mentee's personal tutor. This final step does make the process more formal in that the university will have to act on the information provided, so, although it may be the only outcome, it is perhaps better for the mentee to come to this conclusion herself.

Alison has taken on a new role as head of department in a college and you have been working with her for three months to support the transition to this new role. When you first met Alison you were struck by the strength of her conviction in relation to the purpose of further education. She seemed very passionate about offering opportunities to help people change their lives and felt that her new role would help her to have more control over how individual courses were developed and managed. In her opinion the students were the most important part of the process and were the college's marketing strategy – if students were well trained and competent then in Alison's view that was the best advertisement the college could have.

After being in the role for a few months Alison was beginning to have doubts about her ability to influence curriculum design and management in the way she wanted to. She was

---

overwhelmed by the targets she had been set by senior leaders and by the focus on what she saw as evidencing, rather than improving, performance. Meetings with others in her position indicated that her department's performance was lower than others – on her courses, there were always some students who didn't make the grade – but this wasn't the case in other areas and she was beginning to question if her team were too strict. She didn't know how she could encourage her team to achieve the targets set alongside maintaining the robust assessment process that was important to them.

At your most recent meeting, Alison seemed to have a change of heart and had decided on a number of strategies that she wanted to implement in order to make it easier for students in her department to pass assessments. In her view this would allow her to meet the targets set and would ensure that her department compared favourably with others.

In this case the mentee appears to be questioning her own values and those of her team in order to meet the pressures applied by senior managers. In doing so, she is adjusting the initial reasons for taking on the role in the first place and is trying to rationalise this decision by making comparisons with other departments. The concern is that the mentee seems to be experiencing some cognitive dissonance and this may lead to some decisions that are later regretted.

Cognitive dissonance

In psychology, cognitive dissonance refers to a situation involving conflicting attitudes, beliefs or behaviours, and usually occurs when someone is put into a position of performing an action or making a decision that contradicts their values and beliefs. This produces a feeling of discomfort leading to an alteration in one of the attitudes, beliefs or behaviours to reduce the discomfort felt and restore some sense of balance. For example, you may firmly believe that truth is the foundation of good communication but in your work role are encouraged not to be truthful with others because this is likely to lead to better outcomes for the organisation. Initially being untruthful is challenging and uncomfortable but in order to accommodate this you justify the behaviour on the basis that it supports the organisation you work for and keeps you in a job.

Festinger's (1957) cognitive dissonance theory suggests that we have an inner drive to hold all our attitudes and beliefs in harmony and avoid disharmony (or dissonance), and when there is inconsistency something must change in order to eliminate the dissonance. To do this we need to consider the actions that will reduce the stress we are feeling and can do so in one of three ways:

1. We can change our attitudes and beliefs.
2. We can acquire new information that helps reduce the dissonance.
3. We can use internal reasoning and justification to accommodate the dissonance.

On the surface, doing things that conflict with our values seems unlikely but there are many situations when this happens both personally and professionally. Think about the betrayed wife for whom fidelity in marriage is important – when she discovers her husband's betrayal, her immediate values would suggest that she should end the relationship, but she may choose a different route in order to hold on to some of the other things she values such as companionship, a complete family, financial security, etc. In this case dissonance could be accommodated by a series of justifications that help to reduce the initial discomfort, such as laying blame for the betrayal on another party, normalising the behaviour as a part of long-term relationships and so on.

There may be a number of reasons why people choose to ignore or alter their values in order to do things with which they fundamentally disagree. A key influence is rationalising decisions on the basis that the greater value will be gained through such compromise. Another influential reason is that challenge can be uncomfortable and it is natural for most people to avoid such confrontation. In such cases, the adjustment of one's values and beliefs seems like a logical action.

In the case of Alison the concern is that compromising her values will lead to decisions that she later regrets. She has found an initial solution in making assessments easier to achieve, but does this fit with her team's view of robust assessment and does it have the potential to influence the overall quality of the training received by students? It is important to encourage Alison to reflect on the outcome of her decisions to ensure that she makes choices she doesn't later regret. The following are some strategies you could try:

- Evaluate the journey to the decisions made. This could be done using a shortened version of the symbolic timeline outlined in Chapter 11.

- Use an activity to refer back to core values; there is an activity in Chapter 1 that could easily be adapted for this.

- Use Socratic questioning to elicit information about the rationale and reasons for the change of approach, for example:

  - How do you know this?

  - Can you give me an example of that?

  - What do you think causes . . .?

  - What evidence is there to support what you are saying? How might it be refuted?

John is a new mentee who had just taken on a supervisory role in your organisation. You have been working together for three weeks and, so far, have agreed how you will work together and when you will meet. Other than that you have made no real progress and have not been able to discuss setting any developmental targets because you feel you know very little about him.

John has a succinct communication style, which offers you very limited information. He often makes quite definite statements about events but does not elaborate or provide any detail that may be helpful to you. It is as if he assumes you understand exactly what he is thinking and therefore he can communicate in

> a form of shorthand. You are finding this situation very frustrating and need to find a more effective way of communicating with John if you are to make any progress.

It can be very difficult to work with people who offer you very little information about themselves and this situation can be challenging for the most experienced mentors. You could assume that talking with others is perhaps not John's preferred method of communication and try to make this process easier for him by adopting some more creative approaches, for example:

- The use of stories may emphasise the importance of the mentoring relationship without providing a direct challenge in the form of questioning.
- Create a mind-map together, outlining what John would like to get out of the relationship.
- Try to unravel the meaning behind his shorthand statements using questions linked to the meta model.

Meta model

The meta model recognises the tendency that many of us have to abbreviate what we are saying on the premise that others understand us. To some extent this is an efficient form of communication because it often fits normal conversation patterns and, with people we know well, does not create any particular issues in relation to general understanding. However, by communicating in this way we often omit details that may be useful to the other person and to ourselves in terms of gaining a deeper understanding of our own thoughts.

The meta model (Bandler and Grinder 1975) outlines a set of language patterns that indicate where information had been omitted. The basic premise of the model is linked to Korzybski's idea that 'the map is not the territory' and that the language we use is not necessarily a true reflection of the world around us, but of our perceptions of it.

When using the meta model we are considering three general patterns, which highlight the ways in which key information is omitted:

1. Deletion
2. Distortion
3. Generalisation.

Deletions

Deletions refer to a communication pattern in which the speaker is paying attention to certain parts of their experience and excluding others; they may make a general statement about something being a 'good' or 'bad' thing without providing the detail as to why they believe this. For example, 'There is no communication in this organisation' – this actually tells us very little about how that judgement was made. What does 'communication' mean in this context? Who is not communicating? What would be considered full communication?' Deletions fall into four subcategories which emphasis the specific element being deleted: unspecified nouns/verbs; nominalisations; lack of referential index; and comparative deletion.

Unspecified nouns/verbs: when a thing or action has not been identified, the key here is to identify the specific detail being omitted. So, in the earlier example relating to communication, you might say something like:

• Who is not communicating?
• What is not being communicated?
• What specifically does communication mean in this context?

Nominalisations are verbs made into nouns based on a generalised understanding of something, so in the communication example this might be considered a general term in common usage, but of course the speaker and the listener probably have very different ideas about what 'communication' actually means. Some potential questions here would be:

- How would you like to communicate?
- How is communication happening (or not)?
- What does communication mean to you?

Another form of deletion is the *lack of referential index*, which is just a fancy term for deleting the detail relating to whom or what a particular statement refers. So you might ask questions like:

- Who does this relate to?
- What specifically does this relate to?

A *comparative deletion* occurs when the thing or person something is being compared with is deleted. In this case the listener is unlikely to be clear on what basis a comparison is being made. So, if we go back to the conversation about communication, you might be presented with a statement such as 'communication is worse/ better here' and in this case you could ask either or both of the following questions:

- Better or worse than where?
- Better or worse than what?

Distortions

Distortions refer to things that are represented in a way that reflects the speaker's view of the world. They usually illustrate a view that fits with the speaker's map, so what is experienced is distorted in order to fit with their version of the 'truth'. Distortions are usually not based on evidence but on the stories we present to ourselves in order to ensure that new information sits comfortably with what we already 'know'; as a result they can be very limiting. On the plus side, discovering distortions can be one of the most powerful tools for effective reflection and change. For example, if we have always believed that there are limited life opportunities for us, and then receive job offers or potential new prospects, we may assume these things are not genuine or the source cannot be trusted because they do not fit with our existing view of life's limitations. The opportunities are then ignored or dismissed, the offers disappear and we have once again proved to ourselves that we are right! Distortions represent the things that limit our self-belief, provide barriers to progress and stop us from seeing opportunities. In a way distortions form the structure of our beliefs and underpin how we make rules for ourselves. There are four main ways in which we may distort new information: lost performative; mind reading; cause and effect; and presuppositions.

Lost performative usually relates to a value judgement where the source of the judgement is missing. In some versions of the model this is shown as a deletion to indicate the missing source, but we are also distorting the information in order to fit with our current belief system. A lost performative is something we are all familiar with, even if we don't use the term. It represents a powerful phrase used as a form of judgement and often embodies the many 'shoulds' or 'should nots' we all have in our lives, for example you should clean your house every week, you should have a steady job, you should not cheat, you should not tell lies, etc. In most cases such statements lack detail about the source of the information so we don't know why we should or should not do something. Any sentence that expresses a norm or a rule without stating a source for the judgement is a lost performative. So, who decided that these things were good or bad and why? Some questions to uncover such thinking might include:

- How do you know?
- Who says?
- Should?
- Must?
- Shouldn't?

Mind reading is based on the premise that we know what someone else is thinking. When someone is mind reading they claim to know the thoughts, feelings, intentions or other internal processes of another person. Yet such 'knowing' usually has no reasonable evidence base. Some examples might be: 'I know you don't believe me' or 'I know you are upset about that'. The problem with mind reading is that someone may make a decision based on it, assuming they are correct but in all likelihood misinterpreting a situation and potentially leading to the wrong decision. Some easy challenges to mind-reading statements are:

- How do you know?
- What leads you to believe that?
- How do you know that ... [specific detail]?

Another common form of distortion is *cause and effect* whereby there is the belief that one action leads to another reaction. Again this is based on an assumption and has no evidence base to show the connection. Cause-and-effect statements often reflect a presupposition that people are not in control of their emotional state, so they can be caused to feel in a particular way because of another person's actions, for example 'You make me angry' or 'Your talking is making me anxious'. Such simplistic cause-and-effect patterns are usually applicable only in mechanical rather than emotional systems. Others are not in control of our internal states and therefore cannot 'cause' a particular reaction. Some useful challenges to cause-and-effect statements are:

- How does ... make you ...?
- How do you choose to let ...?
- How specifically does .... 'cause' you to choose ...?

The language we use in normal conversational patterns usually offers only a portion of the meaning behind our words. We may be assuming shared understandings based on *presuppositions*, which are statements whereby an element of information must be assumed (or presupposed) for the statement to be true. Presuppositions are basic assumptions that must be true in order for us to make sense of things, they are in effect distorted assumptions, for example 'She is as bad as all the other managers'. This sentence presupposes that she is 'bad', and that all managers are equally 'bad'. It doesn't really offer specific information about what the statement means for the speaker or what specifically has led them to make this statement. Some ways to challenge this are:

- What leads you to believe . . .?
- What are you assuming to make this true?

Generalisations

A final part of the meta model is the use of generalisations. A generalisation is similar to making a sweeping statement about something, or a group of people, based on the beliefs we have previously generated. For example, a bad experience with a particular race of people may cause someone to generalise the whole race as 'impolite' or 'untrustworthy'. A bad experience with a woman may cause someone to generalise that 'all women are frivolous/selfish/. . .'. Generalisations represent how the speaker sees the world and when challenged can open up new possibilities. There are three types of generalisation: complex equivalence; universal quantifier; and modal operators of necessity and possibility.

Complex equivalence: this is where two experiences are interpreted as the same. This simply means that, in the speaker's view, X = Y, for example 'He is a doctor so he will know'. A useful response to this is to challenge the assumption:

- How exactly does . . . mean that . . .?

Another common generalisation is the use of a *universal quantifier*. This type of statement generalises that the same is true for everyone and statements often include words such as 'everybody', 'all', 'no-one', 'always', 'never'. The easiest way to challenge this type of statement is to re-use the appropriate words, or introduce the idea that there is a possibility for a different experience, for example:

- Never? . . . [alternatively you could use all, no-one, always]
- What would happen if you (he/she) did?

Modal operators of necessity and possibility are generalisations that imply a rule. In the case of necessity, they will refer to rules about things we should, must, should not, must not do. In terms of possibility they usually make reference to things we can, can't, will, won't do. An example might be 'I really want to change my job but I can't' or 'I must not disagree with my boss'. A simple response to this would be:

- What would happen if you did?
- What would happen if you could?

When you first read about this model the amount of information can seem overwhelming. I confess my first thought was 'How will I remember all those labels?'. The good news is it isn't important to do that. When you use the model in a practical way you will find that the most important thing is to really listen to the message and think about an appropriate response. If you 'mislabel' something as a lost performative, rather than a modal operator of necessity, does it really matter? The chances are the person you are communicating with won't know the correct label either, and what is most important is that you keep a natural flow in the conversation through your use of appropriate questions. So, if the question you use at first doesn't help, try a different one – remembering of course that this is a conversation with a natural flow and not a cross-examination.

If you want to test your knowledge of the meta model take a look at the following statements and work out which part of the model they fit, for example deletion, distortion or generalisation – and if you want to try the advanced version pinpoint the specific type of deletion, distortion or generalisation from the appropriate subcategories.

'Arriving late for our date means you don't care.'
'I know you think I am extravagant.'
'Your drawing is better.'

'It's wrong to swear.'
'I must visit my parents on Sunday.'
'We want recognition.'
'It's better to go along with things.'
'She is driving me up the wall.'

Now, try to think of the challenges you would use. You will find the answers at the end of the chapter.

The meta model is a powerful tool for removing the surface structure of communication and, used effectively, can uncover meaning that is helpful for development. A word of warning though; you do need to be careful how you use the questions because they can come across as interrogation! It is important to remember to include 'softeners' such as 'I'm wondering about ...' or 'I am curious that you said ...', or 'I'm interested in ...'. It is also important to have rapport with your mentee before you use this technique.

A sprinkling of magic

In everyday life we are presented with a range of both professional and personal dilemmas and it is easy to get caught up by questions for which there appear to be no obvious answers. This is of course when we need to consider the use of different questions or entirely different methods of supporting others. In a sense this is the heart of mentoring; the flexibility with which the mentor approaches a particular dilemma provides the scope for mentees to find solutions and allows them the autonomy they need to navigate their own development. It is also the key to mentors' development for, without such flexibility, we are unable to have the vision required for change.

In this chapter we have considered a range of dilemmas mentors may face and discussed the potential approaches that might be taken to manage these dilemmas. The strategies suggested are based on

Figure 12.1 A sprinkling of magic: supporting mentees through dilemmas

gaining a better understanding of the thinking that influences mentees' actions in order to make the most informed decisions about
future steps. By learning from our experience we can reflect honestly
on the dilemmas presented before choosing a way forward. It is also
possible to see dilemmas not as problems to be tackled but as
opportunities for growth. Taking inspiration from Nietzsche, this
may challenge each of us to 'Dare to become someone you feared
you'd never be.' (West 2017:13).

Answer to activity

'Arriving late for our date means you don't care.' This is a generalisation and an example of a complex equivalence, based on the idea

that one specific action, that is arriving late, has an equally significant meaning. A potential challenge to this might be 'How does arriving late mean that I don't care?'.

'I know you think I am extravagant.' This is a distortion and an example of mind reading. You don't actually know someone else's thoughts (unless you have special powers) so you could challenge this by saying: 'How do you know?' or 'What leads you to believe that?'

'Your drawing is better.' This is an example of a deletion and is a comparative deletion where the source of comparison is missing, so a simple response would be: 'Better than what?'

'It's wrong to swear.' This is a distortion and an example of a lost performative; it represents a rule without a source and could be challenged by: 'Who says?' or 'How do you know?'

'I must visit my parents on Sunday.' A generalisation and a modal operator of necessity, which could be challenged by: 'What would happen if you didn't?'

'We want recognition.' This is an example of a deletion with a missing source (unspecified verb); we are not actually sure what is meant be recognition so could ask: 'How do you want to be recognised?'

'It's better to go along with things.' This is an example of a distortion in the form of a presupposition. There is an assumption of shared understanding of why this might be a better approach, to challenge this statement you could say 'What leads you to believe that?'

'She is driving me up the wall.' This is another distortion, this time a cause-and-effect one in which a particular action, or in this case a person, is believed to be causing another reaction. A simple challenge for this could be: 'How specifically is she driving you up the wall?'

Suggested further reading

Lancer, N., Clutterbuck, D. and Megginson, D. (2016) *Techniques for Coaching and Mentoring* (2nd edn). Oxon: Routledge.

References

Bandler, R. and Grinder, J. (1975) *The Structure of Magic I: A Book about Language and Therapy*. Palo Alto, CA: Science & Behavior Books.

Clutterbuck, D. (2016) Working with Ethical Dilemmas. Available at: https://coachingandmentoringinternational.org/working-with-ethical-dilemmas/ [date accessed 18 July 2018].

Festinger, L. (1957) *A Theory of Cognitive Dissonance*. Stanford, CA: Stanford University Press.

West, P. (2017) *Get Over Yourself: Nietzsche for Our Times*. Exeter: Imprint Academic Ltd.

Transitions

From seed to sapling and sapling to tree we see the transformation of every arboreal species. Trees develop roots, branches, foliage and flowers until they eventually bear fruit and reproduce themselves. This wonder of nature is not an instant transformation but a slow transition from small seedling to a strong healthy tree, and it requires the right amount of time as well as the appropriate conditions to be successful.

As discussed in previous chapters, mentoring can have a very positive, sometimes life-changing, impact. It can and should represent a relationship that inspires mutual growth and in this way is transformational for both individuals and groups. It is a form of 'magic' but not in the sense of the simple waving of a wand in order to transform one thing into another. The magic of mentoring is a slower, much more subtle alchemy and as such forms part of the process of transition. In this chapter we consider the stages of transition and the mentor's role in providing appropriate support for successful change.

The process of transition

In earlier chapters we discussed the benefits of coaching and mentoring in developing individuals, creating a knowledge culture and enhancing capability. This is often a transformative process for both individuals and organisations, but it should also be recognised as a transition and something that requires support and a period of time to move from one state to another. Without acknowledging and being prepared for this process, it is possible that the benefits of mentoring may not be fully realised and the changes that have taken place through the mentoring relationship are not recognised. There is no magic spell for change; it is not something we can activate at the flick of a switch, nor is it a quick fix. Many of us have learnt this through bitter experience. How many times have you read stories about other people's transformative experiences, those moments when a sudden flash of inspiration gave them THE idea they needed to make their own personal transformation – and how often has this related to your own life? I am making an educated guess (based on my own experiences) that any such transformation was not the result of one moment, or one action, but a process that developed over time. To refer back to Bateson's (1972) work on systems theory and the causal chains that work within systems, it is unlikely there will be one single difference, but quite likely that our memories are attached to specific events that make it seem that way.

Transition is an important part of the mentoring process and the mentor's role in guiding that transition is key to successful change; looking for short cuts may not be the answer. On the contrary, change might be quite easily undone if insufficient time is provided for that change to be integrated into day-to-day practice.

Coping strategies

A woman was in the habit of taking her dog for a walk twice a day in her local park. She noticed a cocoon hanging from the branch of a bush. She wondered how long it would be before the butterfly would emerge.

One day she saw that a small opening had appeared, and she watched, fascinated, for several hours as the butterfly struggled to emerge. After a while the butterfly's progress seemed to slow down, and then movement stopped altogether. It seemed as if the butterfly had become worn out with the effort. So the woman decided to help.

She took a pair of nail scissors from her bag and snipped through the last part of the cocoon. The butterfly slid out easily, but she immediately saw that something was wrong. The butterfly was misshapen. The body was too large and the wings too small. The woman thought this would soon correct itself, but it didn't. All the butterfly could do was crawl around with its swollen body and shrivelled wings. It never flew and soon died.

What this woman didn't understand was the bigger picture. She assumed kindness, compassion and speed would improve the butterfly's development. She didn't understand that the restriction of the cocoon and the effort required for the butterfly to emerge through the tiny aperture are nature's way of forcing fluid from the butterfly's body to its wings. Only when the butterfly has gone through this process in its own time will it be ready for flight.

(Owen 2004:105)

What is the mentor's role in supporting transition? Do you recognise the points at which you must support your mentee's transition and those when you need to permit the struggle? In what ways can intervention both support and limit potential?

Recognising boundaries in mentoring is quite straightforward when we consider situations that may involve ethical judgements, but far less simple when the boundary relates to providing someone with the space to learn. For most mentors this can be something of a dilemma, after all we choose to mentor others because we want to provide support and guidance, so withholding such support seems counterintuitive. But, there are times when the most useful thing you can do is to take a step back and simply allow your mentee the space to learn.

In Chapter 12 we discussed the notion of cognitive dissonance (Festinger 1957) and the ways in which we may resolve this by changing our perceptions or actions. In the first instance, dissonance is viewed as something uncomfortable because it relates to a lack of harmony in thoughts and actions, creating a situation in which we may question one or the other. Although this is uncomfortable it could also be argued that it provides an opportunity for deep learning because it encourages us to reflect on why we feel such discord. New, sometimes unexpected, information is likely to cause some degree of dissonance but the fact that we are cognizant of such dissonance means that we are in a position to choose how we react to it. This is a powerful situation for the mentee to be in and one that needs to be supported but not over-guided by the mentor.

Introducing alligators

One evening an old farmer was walking along a country lane. He looked into a field and saw a group of young women bathing naked in a pond. The women noticed him at about the same time as he noticed them.

One woman shouted, 'We're not coming out till you leave.'

The farmer replied, 'Oh, I'm not here to watch you ladies swimming naked, or running around in the meadow with nothing on. I'm just here to feed the alligator.'

(Owen 2004:103)

Is there ever a time when you need to introduce a few alligators to prompt change? Not all mentees will be naturally curious and not all will have the ability to reflect honestly and openly on their practice. There may be many reasons for this, some of which we have explored in other chapters, and in the overall process of mentoring it is likely that you will utilise a number of techniques in order to increase the potential for change. The introduction of cognitive dissonance, which has the potential to open up other perspectives, may be another technique you could employ. This could be done through your questioning technique, through sharing observations or by introducing a metaphor that prompts thinking. Often short stories, such as the ones introduced in this chapter, are an easy way of de-personalising a situation and approaching a subject in a way that is palatable even to the most resistant of mentees.

Using metaphors effectively

Using stories or metaphors in mentoring can help to highlight things that your mentee may not be fully aware of and as a result may aid understanding of a given situation. Stories use powerful imagery and are often written in ways that capture the imagination, making them a palatable approach, particularly for mentees who may be more reluctant to share information. It may even be possible to place the mentee within the metaphor, or embed the metaphor into reality in order to make the experience more personal. This can be done using the scripted fantasy approach outlined in Chapter 11, in which the mentee would create their own story based on a few prompts (Hall and Leech 1990).

What is important is that time is taken to understand the message and extract learning from the metaphor because this will inform future changes.

The itch, question, goal technique

For mentees who can articulate their concerns, one strategy to help effective transition is the 'itch, question, goal' technique, which provides a structure for recognising and addressing issues that present at a conscious or subconscious level (Lancer et al. 2016). This is linked to reflection and could be incorporated into guided journal activities. The steps are as follows:

- Over a period of time, record any 'itches' experienced. An itch is a sense of discomfort or anxiety about an aspect of work or life.
- At the next meeting, encourage the mentee to order the itches into a number of themes and, for each theme, develop a number of questions.

- Then cluster the questions in order to find a question or questions that provide the scope to delve a little deeper.

- The mentee then asks 'What would I have to do to answer that/ those question(s)?' Finally negotiate one or more goals relating to any issues identified.

This strategy, illustrated in Figure 13.1, helps to bring issues to the surface in a way that puts the mentee in control of the process and provides a structure for setting meaningful goals.

The change transition curve

Change is experienced differently by different people. Some have the ability to sail through life's turbulence whereas others find the slightest ripple to be a significant challenge. However, for most of us the acceptance of significant changes in our lives is more of a journey than a single leap. This is recognised in the change curve, which illustrates the various stages experienced when undergoing fundamental change (Kubler-Ross 2005). Although originally developed in relation to dealing with loss, this model is helpful in aiding our understanding of the process of change and can be applied to a number of situations. The change curve originally recognised five stages to accepting change, but adaptation for use in other contexts has added some stages to the curve. For the purposes of illustrating the behavioural change that often occurs in mentoring, an adapted version of the model has been included in Figure 13.2.

Denial represents the disbelief that a specific change is really happening. This makes a lot of sense in the case of sudden loss such as death but can also be felt in other events such as separation from a loved one or job loss. Typical behaviours at this stage are continuing as if nothing has happened and for some an experience of shame. At work, this might mean continuing to do the job in the same way or, at home, making a meal for the loved one whose departure is imminent. If you have ever watched the film 'The Full Monty' you will recognise a very real example of this when one of the characters dresses to go to work every day, leaves

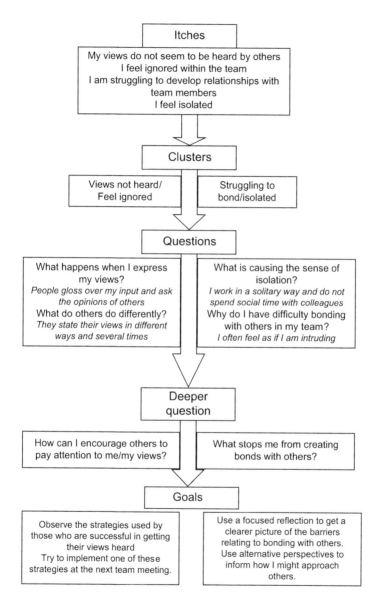

Figure 13.1 The itch, question, goal technique

the house at the same time, lets his wife believe everything is normal, but has actually lost his job; he simply cannot face that fact and is experiencing shame alongside his grief at the loss. At this stage, the mentee needs time to adjust to the change and may simply need to be heard. There is no specific timeframe that should be adhered to, and subsequently no pressure that someone should have 'got over it' by a certain point. It is also helpful if information is provided that aids understanding of what is happening and of what support is available.

Frustration is the recognition that things are different; denial has passed and realisation of the event has hit. This is often accompanied by anger, perhaps looking for someone to blame. Some people may direct the anger at themselves, others will direct it at those around them and, depending on the target, may potentially exacerbate the situation. Mentors can support this stage by listening and providing a safe space for any concerns to be voiced.

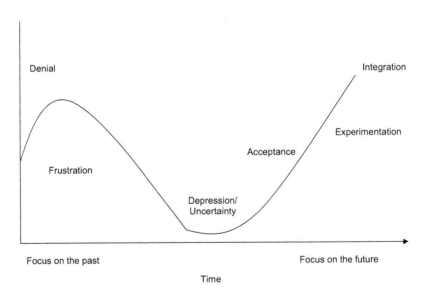

Figure 13.2 The change curve adapted from Kubler-Ross (2005)

Depression/uncertainty is depicted as the lowest point on the curve for obvious reasons. At this stage the person is likely to feel sadness, regret and fear for the future. The journey ahead seems very difficult and people often have limited motivation, sometimes becoming reclusive. Ways to support this phase are to listen to feelings without judgement and trying to reassure the mentee that others have or are experiencing the same feelings. It may be useful to explain the transition curve to provide an illustration that change, and eventual positive change, will continue and that the mentee will not be stuck in this phase indefinitely.

Acceptance that change is happening begins when the realisation that denial is futile occurs. At this stage we become resigned to the situation and accept it fully. Although this is not necessarily a happy place to be, it is the first step to moving on. Ways to support this phase are to help the mentee acknowledge the change and begin to open up discussions about ways forward. It may be possible to use a reframing activity at this point, but be led by the mentee; for some, the journey to acceptance will have been difficult and they will not yet be ready to reframe the experience into something more positive, whereas others may welcome the opportunity to move forward.

Experimentation follows as acceptance grows. Once we have accepted the inevitability of change we are in a better position to explore what that change means for us. Losing our job means we lose the familiarity and comfort that goes with it, but it also opens up opportunities to find something we enjoy more. If the change is the end of a relationship, we may be able to acknowledge that the person/relationship was less than perfect and that now is the time to find someone with whom we are more compatible. Mentors may support this stage by opening up discussions about new opportunities, or where relevant by organising and supporting appropriate training. For those mentees who like to discuss a range of ideas, the creation of a mind-map might be a useful strategy.

Integration is the point at which the change becomes second nature and mentees may even question why they were concerned in the first place! Although this stage requires little support from the mentor, it is important to remember to celebrate the achievement and acknowledge the learning that has taken place in order to reach this stage.

Everyone reacts in different ways to change and may not go through all of the stages in the transition curve. It is also highly likely that they will move through the phases at different paces. For some the step from denial to acceptance is swift; for others it is a long process. The role of the mentor is to be a partner in the journey and to discuss ways forward when the mentee is ready to do so.

Christina seems to have been withdrawn for several weeks and, when asked, says she is simply tired and there is nothing wrong. You know that she has been absent from work quite a lot and, whenever you meet, she seems moody and irritable. Previously she rarely missed a day of work and was considered a very relaxed and sociable person, so this change in behaviour is a concern. Christina finally decides to open up to you and says that the problem is with her colleague who she feels is not trustworthy. According to Christina, this particular colleague has taken some of her work and presented this to the senior team as his own. She is adamant that he is in the wrong and now feels it is very difficult to trust anyone at work.

After further discussion you discover that Christina has also been having some problems at home. Her husband of 10 years has told her that he wants to leave as he has met someone else. In Christina's view this is simply a 'blip' because she is certain he is not serious. She says she is not concerned about this event and that her focus is on making sure that her colleague's 'cheating' is highlighted to others as, in her words, 'he cannot be allowed to get away with this'.

We all have different ways of dealing with emotional conflict and can be in denial about anything that makes us feel vulnerable or threatens our sense of stability. In this case, Christina is not willing to acknowledge the difficulties in her personal life, perhaps because at this point it is too difficult to do so; instead, she is focusing her frustration on a situation in the workplace. In this particular scenario, how would the mentor support progress from the denial and frustration stages of the change curve?

When we are in denial it can be difficult to acknowledge the situation and the actual problem may by downplayed so that we don't have to face it. Although this can seem unhealthy, it is something that mentors need to recognise. It isn't possible, or sensible, to force movement on to the next stage and it is worth considering that a period of denial may actually be useful to allow the difficult information to be absorbed. Keeping discussion open and using a gently probing questioning technique are the best options here because these allow the mentee to address her concerns at a time that is right for her. By being able to discuss things in a safe way, it is likely that realisation will occur and that change will progress to the next stage.

Categories of intervention

As illustrated in the previous case study, it can sometimes be difficult to know how direct you should be in providing support to your mentee. Should you take on a challenging or supporting stance or should your role be focused on nurturing or guiding? As outlined in the models of mentoring in Chapter 1, all of these represent important elements of the role. Heron's (2001) categories of intervention provide a framework that may help. It is based on two basic helping styles, which are referred to as *authoritative* or *facilitative* with further subdivisions outlining the specific approaches.

Authoritative interventions

Authoritative interventions represent types of helping that involve providing information, challenging behaviours or making direct suggestions/providing guidance on the next steps. Interventions that are considered *facilitative* are those that involve drawing out information or ideas, and helping the mentee to reach his or her own decisions. Both are appropriate and it is likely that you will use a range of approaches in different scenarios.

Thinking about your own mentoring practice:

What type of authoritative interventions do you use?
When are you likely to use these?
What type of facilitative interventions do you use?
What leads you to choose these approaches?

In Heron's (2001) model, authoritative interventions include the following:

- *Prescriptive*: whereby you would explicitly guide the behaviour of the mentee by giving either advice or direction. For example, a mentee may be new to the organisation and you set them the task of finding their way around the building and introducing themselves to certain people.

- *Informative*: where you seek to impart knowledge, information or specific instruction. For example, there may be a specific workplace protocol that you choose to guide your mentee through.

- *Confronting*: refers to direct challenges of behaviours and attitudes. This is not about an aggressive confrontation but is where the mentor seeks to raise the consciousness of the mentee about some limiting attitude or behaviour. For example, you may be aware that your mentee always arrives late to meetings and want to raise awareness of the potential issues caused by this behaviour.

Facilitative interventions include:

- *Cathartic*: this approach involves the use of strategies that help the mentee to express thoughts or emotions they may not have previously confronted. For example, your mentee may have a difficult relationship with their boss that is causing them to behave in unhelpful ways. An intervention that opens up discussion about this also provides the opportunity to start to think about how small behaviour changes might help.

- *Catalytic*: this intervention seeks to elicit self-discovery, which leads to self-directed learning and problem solving. For example, you may help your mentee to reflect on their practice and relationships with others in a way that allows them to highlight and find alternatives to limiting behaviours.

- *Supportive*: this involves building confidence in your mentee by focusing on their attributes, competences and achievements. It is part of affirming the worth and value of your mentee which will help build their confidence for further development. By making a point of acknowledging successes and highlighting what is done well, as much as what could be improved, mentors help to create a positive relationship in which mentees can articulate both failures and successes, opening up honest and useful dialogue.

> Kevin is experiencing some difficulties with his new role and has said he thinks he should leave because he feels he isn't doing a 'good enough' job. When you explore this further, Kevin tells you that he likes the work and feels he has a good relationship with the rest of the team, but that his manager more or less ignores him. He has noticed that this isn't the case with other team members because she often talks about what a great job they are doing and continually offers praise or congratulations at team meetings, emphasising their skills and attributes. When his assumptions about the situation are questioned, Kevin says he is certain that this is the case because he has experienced it before. Kevin finds this difficult to talk about but says he has come to the conclusion that he is not good at making an impact, and this must be the case here otherwise his manager would be including him in her circle of praise.

In this case what would be the best type of intervention? Would it be most useful to take an authoritative or facilitative approach?

Kevin seems to be making some assumptions about his manager here, even though he has some 'evidence' on which to base them, but has he really explored what is going on and is there a reason why he is reacting so strongly? Or does this represent an issue that may not actually be to do with the scenario that is being presented? Given that Kevin has mentioned things that have happened before, this may well be the case and it might be useful to use a facilitative approach, which would allow Kevin to unpick some of the reasons behind his own response, in particular a catalytic intervention which would provide the stimulus for self-learning. The meta model outlined in Chapter 12 might be a helpful starting point because this would allow you to explore some of the reasons behind the assumptions.

Prophecy and Pygmalion

In the previous case study, it is clear that the manager, or Kevin's response to the manager, was having a significant impact resulting in the judgement of 'not good enough'. The case study was intended to show that we can misinterpret information through a process of mind reading and that there are strategies a mentor can use to help unpick the assumptions behind this. It may also be an example of a self-fulfilling prophecy whereby a decision has been taken based on expectations of not being good enough, or not making an impact, which in turn affects Kevin's behaviour in such a way that it actually creates the scenario he has imagined. However, what if the manager's actions were a representation of her actual thoughts, what if she genuinely thought that Kevin was not doing a good enough job and was conveying this in a number of subtle ways? Consciously or not we let people know what our expectations of them are by exhibiting a number of cues, some as subtle as the tilting of heads or the raising of eyebrows, and some much more obvious such as ignoring or criticising someone. Inevitably people pick up on these queues and make their own judgements about a situation as a result. If this were the case, would your approach to the situation be any different?

As a mentor the main focus should be the best way in which you can support your mentee. Although it is helpful to think through situations and the reasons behind them, the mentor's role is about supporting a transition rather than analysing a history. As outlined in Chapter 5, the Pygmalion effect provides an example of the impact of our expectations of others. The key principles are as follows:

- We form certain expectations of people or events
- We communicate those expectations with various cues
- People tend to respond to these cues by adjusting their behaviour to match them
- The result is that the original expectation becomes true.

According to the theory, performance is better when greater expectations are placed on individuals (Rosenthal and Jacobsen 1968), and in the example provided our mentee believes that his manager has limited expectations of his performance. If this is the case, is it possible to use the Pygmalion effect to help the mentee to move beyond this barrier? This could be achieved by using a more authoritative intervention, whereby your expectations are made clear and focused targets are used to provide a clear structure for development.

Think about your current relationships with mentees. Are there some for whom you have higher expectations than others? Are there reasons for this? In what ways do you convey these expectations? Are there any other (less direct) ways in which you might be conveying information?

The Pygmalion effect is an interesting phenomenon and demonstrates the power of human interaction. It also provides an example of the real power of mentoring. A mentoring relationship is based on mutual respect and understanding, mentors provide support and guidance and also portray their expectations of mentees in ways that help them to develop beyond current performance or patterns of behaviour.

A sprinkling of magic

Any change involves a process of transition from a previous state to a new state and is something that is experienced by both mentees and mentors. As well as being aware of the need to guide the process for your mentee, it is important to recognise your own transition. For some mentors this may be the transition from novice to expert; for others it is about continuing to develop their expertise, something that can be done only through experiencing and examining your mentoring practice.

In this chapter we have considered the ways in which transitions can be supported through mentoring and have discussed a number of techniques that can be used to help smooth the process. This is a fundamental part of the mentor's role and something that can have a

Figure 13.3 A sprinkling of magic: transition

lasting impact. The acknowledgement of transition as a process helps us to prepare for its lack of immediacy, and facilitates the time required to build confidence in our abilities to achieve whatever we set out to do. The importance of change cannot be underestimated, if we choose to be successful, there is a certain amount of inevitability in it. A the world evolves, so must we in full knowledge that any change requires effort and persistence, as stated by Maya Angelou: 'We delight in the beauty of the butterfly but rarely admit the changes it has gone through to achieve that beauty' (cited in The Guardian online).

Suggested further reading

Owen, N. (2001) *The Magic of Metaphor: 77 Stories for Teachers, Trainers and Thinkers.* Carmarthen: Crown House Publishing Ltd.

References

Bateson, G. (1972) *Steps to an Ecology of Mind.* London: University of Chicago Press.

Festinger, L. (1957) *A Theory of Cognitive Dissonance.* Stanford, CA: Stanford University Press.

Guardian online. Maya Angelou Quotes. Available at: https://www.theguardian.com/books/2014/may/28/maya-angelou-in-fifteen-quotes [date accessed 27 July 2018].

Hall, E. and Leech, A. (1990) *Scripted Fantasy in the Classroom.* London: Routledge.

Heron, J. (2001) *Helping the Client: A Creative Practical Guide* (5th edn). London: Sage Publications Ltd.

Kubler-Ross, E. (2005) *On Grief and Grieving, Finding the Meaning of Grief through the Five Stages of Loss.* London: Simon & Schuster Ltd.

Lancer, N., Clutterbuck, D. and Megginson, D. (2016) *Techniques for Coaching and Mentoring* (2nd edn). Oxon: Routledge.

Owen, N. (2004) *More Magic of Metaphor: Stories for Leaders, Influencers, Motivators and Spiral Dynamics Wizards.* Carmarthen: Crown House Publishing Ltd.

Rosenthal, R. and Jacobsen, L. (1968) *Pygmalion in the Classroom: Teacher Expectation and Pupils' Intellectual Development.* New York: Holt, Rinehart & Winston.

Working with others

Trees are known for their ability to live in supportive communities in which they communicate, look out for each other and share nutrients through their root systems. Trees recognise the power of collaboration and as a result have evolved into self-supporting networks.

In contrast, many mentors work in isolation and do not have the benefit of working within a collaborative network that supports their practice. In this chapter we explore the ways in which communities of professional practice can support the mentoring role and consider how to build a mentoring culture.

Communities of professional practice

In Chapter 2 I discussed the idea of communities of practice (Lave and Wenger 1991) to introduce the ways in which learning can take place through social interaction. A community of practice can be any group that has a shared interest or identity in relation to a common domain and is often found in professional groups. Communities of practice could also be referred to as communities of learning because they provide an opportunity for members to collaborate through the sharing of knowledge and resources, as well as creating a forum for discussion. They are a resource in terms of their ability to provide up-to-date information, as well as a source of support for individuals. Being a part of a community also provides a sense of meaning and belonging because within this space you will be sharing with others who understand your experiences.

How do communities of practice work?

Communities of practice (CoP) are centred around a particular domain, an identity that is shared for all participants, for example you may find a CoP among a group of nurses, researchers or Trekkies (devotees of Star Trek). Membership of the CoP involves a commitment to the particular domain and a willingness to share in its activities, which according to Wenger consist of 'mutual engagement', 'joint enterprise' and 'shared repertoire' (Wenger 1998:72–73).

It is assumed that, by choosing to be part of the CoP, members will build collaborative relationships, tying them together as a group in a form of mutual engagement. This term refers to the pattern of inter-action within the community as well as the amount of interaction, and may vary according to the type of community. For example a group of health practitioners may meet formally once a month, whereas Trekkies could interact through an online community that has a less formal structure. Through the type, formality and regularity of their interactions the group shapes both its practice and its culture.

A shared understanding of what connects the CoP, the purpose that binds the group together, is a process of negotiation and involves negotiated goals, a clear understanding of the structure of the group and a sense of mutual accountability. In some ways this is like a mission statement but not one that is provided for the community by others; it is a shared mission based on mutual negotiation.

Shared repertoire refers to the development and maintenance of procedures, techniques, jargon, symbols, actions, concepts, etc. The CoP will have a shared history because the repertoire is shaped by the participants, giving the CoP its own identity. The shared repertoire may also include specific language relating to the community. Just think about joining a new group at work and experiencing your very first meeting – this often involves deciphering the language that is in common usage among the group such as acronyms for particular processes, names for specific roles and so on. Through their interactions the CoP creates a shared understanding of both what connects them and how this is communicated.

Benefits of communities of practice

We come across communities of practice in all areas of our life, although they may not always be given that name – in almost every organisation and between organisations, in communities, in professions and trades. The ubiquity of the practice suggests that there are many benefits to involvement and a few of these have been outlined in Table 14.1.

In essence a CoP is a forum within which participants can share and extend knowledge and enjoy the practical benefits of cooperative enquiry. They also provide a support network for practitioners, which in turn removes the isolation experienced by those who work in solitary domains.

Table 14.1 Benefits of communities of practice

Benefits of communities of practice	Example
Problem solving	'Can we work on this together and brainstorm some ideas?'
Requests for information	'Where can I find . . .?'
Seeking experience	'Has anyone dealt with . . .?'
Reusing assets	'I have a proposal I wrote last year . . .. I can send it to you and you can re-tweak it if you like.'
Coordination and synergy	'Can we combine our purchases to achieve a bulk discount?'
Building an argument	'How do people elsewhere do this?'
Growing confidence	'Before I do this I want to run it by you . . .'
Discussing developments	'What do you think of the new . . . does it work?'
Visits	'Can we come and look at . . . we need to set up something similar.'
Mapping knowledge and identifying gaps	'What are we missing? What other groups can we connect with?'

Think back on your own professional experience, in particular to times when you experienced difficulty. What sort of support was available? What type of support would have been helpful to you?

Were there times when you felt a little lost and just needed someone with whom to talk things through? Were you ever confused by some aspect of your practice and would have benefited from the experience of others? Were you always aware of the opportunities available to you and the particular path you wanted to take? All of these are typical questions that we struggle with and are questions that are easily answered by people who have experience of your particular domain.

Divya is an early career researcher at a university. She is keen to carry out research in an unusual field in which there is limited expertise in her department and the university as a whole. Divya is struggling to get started on her research because she is not yet clear on the research landscape for her area of interest. She is becoming increasingly worried that she may be pursuing something that is not feasible and says she really needs to be in contact with people who can guide her.

Being part of a relevant CoP would certainly be of help to Divya but, as this is not your area of expertise, how would you help her to find the right source of support? Communities of practice are all based on networking, so the first step when trying to locate the right CoP is to speak to people interested in the same, or a related domain. If there were someone in the university who studied a similar topic, they would be the first port of call because they are likely to be aware of the associated professional bodies, which in turn will have details of any special interest groups who may be of help. A little investigative work and some perseverance are all that is required.

Communities of practice for mentors

Like any other group, mentors can benefit from being involved in a CoP. Many organisations set up formal or informal groups to provide this forum, although they may not necessarily have the same name. For example, mentors working with trainee teachers will usually be invited to take part in network meetings set up by the body organising the training qualification, and coaches and mentors working within businesses are likely to have a group or committee set up to discuss the overall practice within the organisation. These certainly offer opportunities to share expertise and get some of your questions answered but it is possible that they won't meet all of your development needs. It may be worth exploring the opportunities available externally in order to widen the knowledge base to which you have access. A good starting point is to contact the professional bodies linked to your area of practice and find out what is available; often these may be referred to as support networks, or special interest groups but are generally operated along the lines of a CoP. It is also useful to look out for training and networking events in relation to mentoring because these will provide an opportunity to meet with other mentors working in a range of settings. Organisations such as the European Mentoring and Coaching Council might be a good starting point because they offer access to conferences, newsletters and communities of practice, and have a framework for accreditation. There are also a number of online forums that may be useful, and searching networks such as those provided by LinkedIn or Twitter might be helpful.

Create a list of organisations that may provide access to relevant communities of practice. List the ways you can enhance your professional development as a coach or mentor by accessing these networks.

Sharing knowledge and enhancing creativity

According to Csikszentmihalyi (1996) creativity can be defined as: 'any act, idea, or product that changes an existing domain or that transforms an existing domain into a new one' (1996:28). This recognises that creativity is not necessarily about creating something completely new but may simply be about seeing something in a different way. According to Robinson (2017) our way of seeing the world is very influenced by our interactions with other people and, citing Geertz, suggests that: 'All human lives are suspended in "webs of significance" that we ourselves have spun' (Robinson 2017:170). Within these webs we find the structure for our individual world-views, which produces a map used to guide our life. As discussed in previous chapters, such maps form the basis of how we interact with others, deal with information, make decisions and so on. They are helpful in providing a framework from which to operate but they also include some distortions or even blanks, areas of unexplored, possibly incorrectly mapped, territory. According to Robinson, 'Creativity is how these threads are formed and woven into the complex fabrics of human culture' (Robinson 2017:170) and, moreover, it is about: 'Making connections [and is] usually driven more by collaboration than by solo efforts' (Robinson 2017:180).

Sharing knowledge is important in encouraging creative practice because it allows us to extend our webs of significance and provides the scope for perspective change. There are also a number of practical benefits:

- It speeds up the process of learning: we can explore something alone until we are familiar with the topic, we can experiment with new ideas and enhance our learning through trial and error, or we can use other people's experiences to inform our own ideas and save the time and effort involved in the period of trial and error.

- It gives us the confidence to innovate: this is difficult to do if we aren't familiar with the landscape and sharing knowledge with others provides information about this. If we know what is out there, we also know what the gaps are. If you have ever seen the programme 'The Dragon's Den' you will be familiar with this idea; there is nothing more embarrassing than a potential entrepreneur who does not know the market and is asking for investment for a product that already exists.

- It alleviates the loss of expertise from staff turnover: if you have access to a CoP you will also have access to the knowledge that may have been lodged with one or two people in an organisation who have now moved on.

- It highlights what we know: often in organisations expertise is not shared as effectively as it could be. The hierarchy sometimes creates a situation whereby knowledge is perceived to be with a few individuals and expertise elsewhere is often not acknowledged or in the full awareness of decision makers.

- It helps us keep up with change: with the best will in the world it can be difficult to keep on top of your area, so having a forum where knowledge is openly shared removes the risk of missing out on key changes.

Developing creativity is often associated with providing flexibility and space to think; however, the power of interaction with others should not be overlooked. According to Davis et al. (2012) collaboration is a key ingredient for the creative environment and they stress the importance of 'liberating innovative relationships' (Davis et al. 2012:179) in enhancing the creative process. Creativity is viewed as a collective action that can be progressed through activities such as brainstorming, consultation or group work, dispelling the myth of the tortured artist who has the sole claim to being creative.

Professional development

In Chapter 1, and throughout this book, a democratic model of mentoring has been advocated. This means that the process of mentoring should be enriching for the mentor and mentee alike, and both should be provided with the opportunity to reflect on, question and enhance their practice in a supportive environment. In this way, effective mentoring becomes a 'duet' where both mentor and mentee help to create a harmonic relationship that enhances the practice of both parties. For this to work effectively, both need to develop a dependency on each other based on relational trust, which includes:

• Respect: showing a genuine commitment to listen to and respect each other's views

• Regard: developed through the relationship as trust builds

• Competence: having confidence in each other's ability to play their part

• Integrity: being honest and behaving ethically (Bryk and Schneider 2002).

Mentors also need to be aware of their own development needs as well as those of their mentees; this means becoming actively aware of areas for development as well as seeking opportunities to enhance skills.

Evaluating mentoring practice

It is very easy to leap at every opportunity for professional development but, in order to make the most of the opportunities, it makes sense to be selective. After all, you only have so much time and there is a danger of spending time on activities that do nothing to enhance your expertise and simply absorb time that could be usefully employed elsewhere. When planning your own professional development, a good place to start is evaluating your current practice. There are a number of strategies that can be used as a basis for evaluation such as a model of reflection like the critical lenses model outlined in Chapter 11, or something specifically related to the coaching or mentoring context. The critical lens model (Brookfield 1995) suggests critically analysing a situation from four different perspectives: the autobiographical, the participants, colleagues and theory. So you might ask yourself:

- How do I feel about my mentoring practice?
- How would my mentees view it?
- What would colleagues say?
- How does my practice relate to theoretical perspectives?

Based on this evaluation what conclusions could you draw about your practice? You may have decided that you are reasonably confident in your practice and that mentees seem to respond well to you but that colleagues might be able to highlight gaps in your knowledge. This evaluation would lead you to explore ways in which you could enhance your own theoretical knowledge in order to improve your mentoring practice. Alternatively you could develop a series of questions specifically related to your practice which allow you to reflect at regular intervals, for example:

- What went well?
- What could have been better?
- What was the level of rapport?
- How well were boundaries respected?
- How did I feel about the meeting?
- How did the mentee seem to feel about the meeting?
- What progress is the mentee making?
- Were there any points in the meeting when I was not confident in my ability?
- Was there anything I could have handled differently?
- What would my mentor say about the meeting?

The final note in this list relates to the perspective of your own mentor. By working with another mentor, who may operate in a supervisory or mentoring capacity, you also have access to another form of evaluation.

Practitioner research

An alternative type of professional development comes in the form of practitioner research. This type of research is led by practitioners in a particular field, for example nurses carrying out research on elements of the nursing role. It is typically carried out for the purpose of advancing practice and as a result tends to be action based. Often, although not always, done in collaboration with others, this type of research offers the opportunity to explore a very specific area of interest and is particularly useful when there is a hypothesis about something that could be improved.

What is unique to this type of research is that it is conducted by people who assume a dual role both as a practitioner and as a researcher, and as such it offers the opportunity not only to reflect on practice but also to apply systematic enquiry to it.

Caitlin has been working as a lecturer and a mentor in a large city university for several years, and during this time has set up a community of practice for mentors who support new members of academic staff. This move was welcomed by the senior management team because it has been very successful in promoting the purpose of mentoring. It has also provided an opportunity for the sharing of good practice as well as a forum for discussing particular concerns.

One recurring concern for Caitlin is the way that mentors are being selected across the university. Over the past two years she has noticed that the new mentors joining the group are often quite inexperienced teachers with limited mentoring expertise. Most have been selected on the basis of teaching evaluations done by heads of department, all of whom are evaluating teaching based on a set of criteria produced by the Quality Directorate.

These new mentors have very definite ideas about what the academic role involves and seem to be inflexible in their views of this. Caitlin is concerned that this rigidity will not be helpful to all mentees. In addition, she is concerned that such a rigid approach will in turn influence new teachers and create a very narrow view of the teaching role and not one that will necessarily meet the needs of students.

In what ways would practitioner research be helpful here? Caitlin's concerns relate to the overall impact of mentoring on teaching within the university so this is very much a focus of her practice both as a member of the academic staff and as a mentor. By implementing a research project she could explore if her hypothesis were correct and generate some ideas about how best to address this problem. The benefit of this is that the research would be very focused on both the role and the organisation so it would have a practical use. Its publication would also highlight a potential problem (or not, depending on the outcome), which could be used to enhance the current mentoring scheme.

In addition to the very pragmatic uses of practitioner research, the act of implementing a research project is very beneficial to the researcher who has the opportunity to explore the literature on the subject and test out ideas in a systematic way. It also provides a forum for networking with others through presentation of the research findings.

Developing a mentoring culture

A mentoring culture is one in which the process of mentoring is embedded within an organisation. It becomes part of a whole organisation approach, which means that it is present at all levels and requires the facilitation of a number of mentoring opportunities as well as the support mechanisms that will aid success.

A mentoring culture may be something that evolves in an informal way or is part of the formal structure within an organisation. Informal mentoring is usually organised at an individual level and not subject to any organisational monitoring. Although this has the benefit of not being hindered by a range of processes, it is also likely to be quite variable and may be less inclusive than something set up at an organisational level.

A formal mentoring scheme will be aligned to an organisation's values and overall mission and will be embedded into practice throughout the organisation. For mentoring in the workplace this is an appropriate model and one that has the benefit of support from organisational policies, monitoring frameworks and funding. In all likelihood mentoring schemes may well fall somewhere on a continuum between the informal and formal, unless it is something an organisation has set up from the very beginning of its existence and is therefore fully embedded in its values and mission statement.

In order to develop a culture of mentoring it is important that there is a shared understanding of the purpose and practice of mentoring within a given context. This means addressing and making clear key points such as:

- Who is entitled to a mentor?
- How are mentors and mentees matched?
- What time is provided for mentoring to happen?
- How long should mentoring last?
- What are the boundaries of the mentoring relationship?
- What happens when the mentoring relationship does not work?
- Is there a mentoring agreement?
- How is mentoring monitored?
- What training is given?
- Is there any formal accreditation for mentors?
- How are mentors supported?
- How is mentoring aligned to the organisation's objectives?

It is also important that mentoring is visible within the organisation. As an activity it can have the feel of something that is done 'behind closed doors' and of course confidentiality does need to be maintained within the relationship. However, the overall purpose and value of mentoring is something that should be communicated widely. If it is more visible, it is more likely to become accepted as something that happens across the organisation.

To ensure a level of consistency in access to mentor support and the support itself, it is important to build in some form of monitoring of mentor activity. There is of course a danger here depending on how this activity is managed. A simple approach would be to produce guidelines as to what is expected within the mentoring framework and align these to a system of monitoring. This will provide one part of the picture but it is also important that those monitoring the activity recognise the very nuanced nature of mentoring and are not tempted to take a 'one-size-fits-all' approach to its assessment. Therefore a more fluid system of monitoring would be a better fit. This in turn will receive criticism in that it is more subjective than something that is measured against set criteria, so it is likely that not everyone will be happy with this approach and that some negotiation is required to set up a form of monitoring that is appropriate.

Mentoring should be a developmental activity and for this reason it should adopt a democratic approach. This means that mentors and mentees should benefit from being involved in mentoring, and this should be recognised within the overall framework. Some ideas for doing this are as follows:

- Provide a support network for mentors through supervision or group support

- Consider the use of an accredited framework to provide recognition of mentoring expertise

- Provide time for mentors' personal and professional development

- Encourage mentors to reflect on their practice and take ownership of their development needs.

The creation of a mentoring culture provides the impetus for change and helps build the confidence required to make that change happen. Perhaps, most important of all, this requires the recognition that mentoring can be a magical process that has within its power the ability to enable transformation at personal and professional levels.

A sprinkling of magic

The advantages of mentoring and the ways in which the process can support change in mentees are quite difficult to dispute but the benefits available to mentors are less widely acknowledged. The development of mentors' skills and confidence is a key aspect of a democratic model of mentoring and as such should be embedded in the overall framework of mentoring, something that can be achieved through the introduction of mentoring cultures and communities of practice.

Similar to the communities of trees in the forest, communities of mentors can work together in ways that provide a strong support network, enhance communication and share knowledge. Through such networks success is demonstrated in playing a symphony rather than a solo, with the potential to produce a whole new composition!

Figure 14.1 A sprinkling of magic: community of practice

Suggested further reading

Wenger-Trayner, E. and Wenger-Trayner, B. (2015) Communities of Practice, A Brief Introduction. Available at: http://wenger-trayner.com/wp-content/uploads/2015/04/07-Brief-introduction-to-communities-of-practice.pdf [date accessed 30 July 2018].

References

Brookfield, S. (1995) *Becoming a Critically Reflective Teacher*. San-Francisco, CA: Jossey-Bass.

Bryk, A. S. and Schneider, B. L. (2002) *Trust in Schools*. New York: Russell Sage Foundation.

Csikszentmihalyi, M. (1996) *Creativity: Flow and the Psychology of Discovery and Invention*. New York: Harper Perennial.

Davis, J. M., Aruldoss, V., McNair, L. and Bizas, N. (2012) Enabling Creativity in Learning Environments: Lessons from the CREANOVA Project. *LEARNing Landscapes*, 6(1): 179–200. Available at: http://sro.sussex.ac.uk/49395/.

Lave, J. and Wenger, E. (1991) *Situated Learning: Legitimate Peripheral Participation*. Cambridge: Cambridge University Press.

Robinson, K. (2017) *Out of Our Minds, the Power of being Creative* (3rd Edn). London: John Wiley & Sons Ltd.

Wenger, E. (1998) *Communities of Practice: Learning, Meaning, and Identity*. Cambridge: Cambridge University Press.

The magic within

The world is full of magical things. We are surrounded by the miraculous, embroidered into the ordinary events of everyday life. We may choose to notice, or continue to let them pass us by.

In his book *The Alchemist*, Paul Coelho tells the tale of a young shepherd from Andalusia who, while sleeping near a sycamore tree by an abandoned church, has a recurring dream about finding buried treasure if he travels to the Egyptian Pyramids. The boy decides to set out on a journey to find the treasure. Along the way he meets a range of mysterious characters and learns many things about the world, including how to listen to the desert and recognise the omens provided by nature. Eventually he arrives at the Egyptian pyramids and begins to dig. He finds nothing. He meets two thieves who rob him and, in the hope that it will save him from death, he tells them about his dream. One of them recounts his own dream about buried treasure – beneath a sycamore tree, next to an abandoned church in Andalusia. (Coelho 1993).

This allegorical tale is intended to be about finding our destiny but the most important message seems to be about how much we learn on life's journeys. As the tale meanders we explore the intentional and more often unintentional learning that takes place for the protagonist. At times it feels frustrating until we eventually discover that many of the events shaped an important experience from which much was learned. The young shepherd is presented with numerous examples of mentoring, none of them providing the answers but each of them showing the way. Ultimately, what he required was already within him, but would he have been able to access this without the journey?

In the tale of the alchemist and throughout this book the tree has provided an illustration of the power of learning and communication. Trees have strong roots that offer nourishment and a solid trunk from which to grow branches and foliage. They are effective communicators and they are adept at functioning within a particular context. Trees work together as part of an intelligent community; they may even be the source of buried treasure. They have much in common with mentors. In addition, trees are in their own right quite magical:

> Since time immemorial and on every possible level, human culture has been inextricably interwoven with the presence of trees. Indeed, the spiritual connection between humans and trees is sacred, primordial, intimate and enduring. Beyond the simple fact that we can't survive without them, we turn to them to restore our harmonizing connection to the earth, we look to them to fuel our inspiration, and we rely on them to keep us sane.
>
> (Whitehurst 2017:1)

Our journey

This book was intended to provide a basic map of the journey to becoming a mentor. Many of the strategies introduced will help you to create a positive, nurturing and productive framework for mentoring, within which both mentor and mentee can flourish. Some of the suggestions may appeal to you and have immediate use and others will inevitably seem less appealing. This is not a concern. My own experience has taught me that ideas and concepts I struggled with are often the ones I needed to explore further. They represented a hurdle I wasn't quite ready to clear but when visited years later proved to be much more relevant than I had first imagined. Have an open mind. The map is only part of the journey; the rest is unique to you.

In Chapter 9 we discussed neurolinguistic programming's (NLP's) presuppositions which included: *We have all the resources we need to succeed or we can create them*. This statement is also a key premise of this book and the strategies outlined within it are aimed at helping mentors and mentees to be more resourceful. This does not mean always finding quick solutions to our problems; rather it refers to developing the ability to find innovative ways to overcome difficulties. Resourcefulness in mentoring means taking the time to recognise real and imagined limitations, having the required persistence to work with them, and using our knowledge and expertise to make the changes necessary to achieve the outcomes we want. We can do this by making use of many of the strategies outlined in the preceding chapters and by creating a nurturing environment that encourages open and honest communication.

Most of all we do this by our ability to be flexible, to recognise the value of different approaches, and to have the confidence and humility to acknowledge that we may not yet have the answers. This type of resourcefulness is an individual state, something we can call upon to help us to change the way we both *do* and *think about* things.

Another key resource we all have access to is our ability to change our perceptions, a skill that helps us to challenge emotions and develop a more positive mindset. Similarly the way that we articulate our faith in others' abilities can have a positive or negative effect (Dweck 2006; Rosenthal and Jacobsen 1968). Whether Pygmalion or prophecy, the stories we create for ourselves have a powerful impact on our ability to achieve. As illustrated by Barrie in his magical tale of Peter Pan: 'The moment you doubt whether you can fly, you cease for ever to be able to do it' (Barrie n.d.).

A democratic approach

Part of the magic of mentoring is the forum it provides to pay attention to the detail, to reflect on our experiences, to notice the ordinary, to recognise patterns, limitations and opportunities. In doing so we can create a different map to guide the personal understanding of our individual journeys. To see the mentoring process as magical is to notice the connection it has to personal and professional development for both *mentor* and *mentee*. By representing the relationship as a shared experience between professionals, as opposed to the archetypal master and apprentice view, the focus shifts from a typically hierarchical relationship to something more balanced, and generates an emphasis on creating the right environment for change as opposed to instruction on what or how to change.

A sprinkling of magic

Taking a democratic approach to mentoring removes the power imbalance usually present in formalised mentoring programmes and advocates a model in which mentors and mentees work together to

Figure 15.1 A sprinkling of magic: the door to 'buried treasure'

facilitate change. With one person no longer being labelled as the 'expert' this also creates a relationship based on mutual respect and trust, and provides both parties with the opportunity to open up their practice to scrutiny and enhancement. A democratic framework places equal value on both the mentor's and the mentee's participation, and is a way of acknowledging that all participants within a relationship bring something to it. It represents a form of collaborative, learning that is supported through reciprocal interactions.

It is accepted that the role of the mentor is a complex balance of many skills, but it is also a symbiotic relationship in which mentors not only share their expertise but continue to develop it through the practice of mentoring. The mentoring process should not begin and end with the mentor's knowledge; learning should be universal and continuous because without this facility we are unlikely to look beyond our current map and might miss out on buried treasure!

A mentor provides the conditions in which a mentee can thrive, a mentor offers guidance and encouragement and they do not have all the answers. By working together both mentors and mentees become part of a bigger system which creates the opportunity for transformational change. Transformation isn't something the mentor does; it is simply a by-product of collegiate practice that creates the conditions in which all can flourish. In a sense, the mentor's role is simply helping the mentee to find their own treasure. As stated by Rowling (2008): 'We do not need magic to transform our world. We carry all the power we need inside ourselves already.'

That's Magic!

References

Barrie, J. M. (n.d.) Peter Pan Quotes. Available at: https://www.goodreads.com/work/quotes/1358908-peter-pan [date accessed 4 August 2018].
Coelho, P. (1993) *The Alchemist*. London: HarperTorch.
Dweck, C. (2006) *Mindset: The New Psychology of Success*. London: Random House Publishing.
Rosenthal, R. and Jacobsen, L. (1968) *Pygmalion in the Classroom: Teacher Expectation and Pupils' Intellectual Development*. New York: Holt, Rinehart & Winston.

Rowling, J. K. (2008) The Fringe Benefits of Failure and the Importance of Imagination. Speech at the Commencement Address at the Annual Meeting of the Harvard Alumni Association. Available at: www.jkrowling.com/en_GB/#/timeline/harvard-commencement-address [date accessed 29 June 2015].

Whitehurst, T. (2017) *The Magic of Trees*. St Paul, MN: Llewellyn Publications.

Index